SPIRITUAL HEALING:
A Patient's Guide

EILEEN INGE HERZBERG

SPIRITUAL HEALING:
A Patient's Guide

INDEX COMPILED BY LYN GREENWOOD

SAFFRON WALDEN
THE C. W. DANIEL COMPANY LIMITED

First published in Great Britain in 1988 by Thorsons.

This completely revised, enlarged and edited edition
published in 1998 by
The C. W. Daniel Company Limited
1 Church Path, Saffron Walden
Essex CB10 1JP, United Kingdom

ISBN 0 85207 308 9

The production of this book was organised by Nicky Clarke of MBC
Print Consultancy, Hadleigh, Suffolk. It was designed and typeset in
Times New Roman by Linda East & Michael Shaw.
Printed and bound by J.W. Arrowsmith of Bristol, England.

ACKNOWLEDGEMENTS

Many thanks to the people who helped me write the third edition of this book—particularly my publisher, Ian Miller, who made it possible. Thanks, Ian, for your enthusiasm, patience, encouragement, Dundee cake and haggis.

Thanks also to Don Copland at the National Federation of Spiritual Healers, Reiki Master Beth Holman, and everyone else who helped me with this edition. I would also like to thank again all the people who helped me with the original version of the book, particularly Jesa Macbeth who was one of the first people to introduce me to the world of spiritual healing. She has been a huge support and inspiration to me over the years. Thank you, Jesa. Special thanks also the the Bristol Cancer Help Centre—particularly Pat and Christopher Pilkington and Dr Rosy Daniel.

Dedicated to my aunt,
Ingeborg Franziska Herzberg,
who died in Auschwitz, aged 12.

CONTENTS

INTRODUCTION TO THE THIRD EDITION

In the decade since this book was first published, spiritual healing has gained much more acceptance amongst the medical profession and the world at large. People can now receive healing in doctors surgeries and hospitals and many healers now work side by side with doctors, in fact many doctors, nurses and other members of the medical Profession also practise healing.

If your doctor has suggested you may benefit from spiritual healing or if you are simply intrigued by the idea, I very much hope that this book will answer all your questions. My aim is to help people who would like to know a little bit about the subject before they try it out.

In writing this book I have had to be selective because I want to demystify spiritual healing. I have tried to keep the book as uncomplicated as possible as spiritual healing itself is simple and straightforward.

My interest in spiritual healing started some 10 years ago when I went on a year-long holiday travelling around America. When I reached San Diego, someone gave me a copy of *Joy's Way* by Dr Brugh Joy which describes his healing experiences (J. P. Tarcher, Los Angeles, 1979). It fired me with enthusiasm to learn more and changed my life for the better.

I hope this book has the same effect on you.

Spiritual Healing –
The Cover Story

WARNING: THIS BOOK CAN SERIOUSLY CHANGE YOUR LIFE

A few years ago, I gave my friend and neighbour, Fay, a copy of my migraine book. I wanted the book to heal her migraines—and it worked! She didn't have another migraine from the moment I gave her the book. I was impressed. The book is called *The Natural Way With Migraine* (published by Element, 1994) and I wondered which particular part of the book had been most help-ful. Fay said: "Oh no, I haven't *read* it, I just stopped getting migraines after you gave it to me."

As you'll discover later in this book, it's the intention that is important—and when I gave Fay the book, I really intended her to stop suffering from migraines, and that was what counted. It will be interesting to see what happens with this book—or rather, this *edition* of the book. This edition has a special front cover, a front cover which comes with a strong healing intention.

The "Healing Goddess" on the front cover comes from a painting by Brian Froud[1]. Brian explains: "It started when my son Toby was about 5. I used to wait at the garden gate and prayed for a few moments when he went off on the school bus. It started off as praying for his safe return, then for his journey in life, and it became a prayer for all children to have a safe journey through their lives. After several years I became aware of a figure of light, a guardian at the gate, over-seeing the threshold. I paint-ed the guardian at the gate, and then another figure of light came to me, and that was the Healing Goddess."

When Brian painted the Healing Goddess, he felt that the

image should be used for healing in the world. It wasn't enough to sell the painting and have just one person benefit from it; he wanted it to be used for healing by whoever needed it, so he had this healing presence printed on postcards and gave them away. When I asked if the Healing Goddess could be used on the front cover of this book he was delighted—it was another way for the image to bring healing to people.

Of course, you can just shrug your shoulders and dismiss the whole idea – or you can pause, sit upright in your chair, take a couple of deep breaths, relax and have a look at the picture on the cover. After a few moments you may want to close your eyes, but still imagine that the picture is in front of your eyes, and carry on breathing slowly and deeply. Allow the Healing Goddess to communicate with you—this may come in words, feelings or just a sort of inner knowing. When you feel ready, take another couple of deep breaths, stretch your fingers and toes and open your eyes. Feel better? Okay, now you've experienced spiritual healing, you can read about it.

[1] Brian Froud created the best-selling "Faeries" and worked with Monty Python's Terry Jones on "Lady Cottington's Pressed Fairy Book". Incidentally, he also designed the Jim Henson films "Dark Crystal" and "Labyrinth". Watch out for Brian Froud's latest offering, "Good Faeries/Bad Faeries" which is due out soon.

CHAPTER 1

WHAT IS SPIRITUAL HEALING?

Spiritual healing can be looked at from several different perspectives: to a priest, spiritual healing comes from God; to a scientist, spiritual healing is a measurable phenomenon of altered brain wave patterns; to a nurse it might be Therapeutic Touch; and to a patient it might be a slim straw to grasp at.

Spiritual healing itself is very simple and straightforward. In fact, it is easier to practise than to describe since the experience speaks for itself and there is no problem then with language.

One of the best descriptions of spiritual healing that I have found came from Dr Alec Forbes, one of the fathers of modern holistic medicine in Great Britain. He said: 'Spiritual healing reaches the parts that other therapies don't reach.' And, as Canon Christopher Pilkington, a healer, trustee and co-founder of the Bristol Cancer Help Centre explains, 'It is spiritual in the sense that it reaches down to the spiritual roots of the personality. The aim of spiritual healing *is* that there should be total healing.'

Scientists might be rivetted by such sophisticated terms as energy transfers through bioplasmic or electromagnetic fields, but that is so much gobbledegook unless you happen to enjoy jargon. And, while 'the power of prayer' might be an 'in' phrase for those of a religious turn of mind, it is an instant turnoff if you are not that way inclined. For many people the very words 'spiritual healing' smack of weird goings on. Before going into any detail about what spiritual healing *is*, perhaps it is just as well to describe what it is *not*.

Spiritual healing is not Spiritualism, any more than it is Catholicism or any other ism. The confusion arises because of the word 'spiritual', which may have all sorts of connotations. Of course, it is very hard to tell the difference between one thing and another if you have never experienced either, so it might help to dispel some myths by explaining who does what and how and why.

First, looking at the *Concise Oxford Dictionary* definition, Spiritualism is the 'belief that departed spirits communicate with and show themselves to men, especially at seances'. The very word 'seance' is enough to make some people run away in horror. But life is not that simple and certainly does not follow pat dictionary definitions. Drawing aside the metaphorical lace curtains, and turning on the lights to take a closer look, we can see that Spiritualism, like many religions, is based on the idea that there is life after death. Where the Spiritualists differ from other religions is that they use mediums to channel messages between this world and the next. I am sure that many people receive comfort and reassurance from the messages they receive through mediums but that is very different from actually healing the sick.

Mediumship is also very different from healing but, having said that, healing does happen within the Spiritualist movement and, as such, is one of the many types of spiritual healing on offer.

Just as physical healing addresses itself to the nuts and bolts of the body, so spiritual healing is essentially concerned with spirit. It is the word 'spirit' that can be tricky.

Every word we use has its own power, its own magic. The word 'spirit' is more charged with meaning than most, which makes it more difficult to pin down with precise definitions. We use the word 'spirit' all the time without thinking—fighting spirit, team spirit, high spirits, low spirits... We instinctively feel these forms of 'spirit' without necessarily being able to explain what they are.

According to the *Little Oxford Dictionary*, spirit means animating or vital principle. The *Concise Oxford Dictionary* uses longer words—it describes spirit as the intelligent or immaterial part of man, the soul. The *Concise Oxford Dictionary* says that soul is also the immaterial part of man. Just flicking through *Roget's Thesaurus* shows up some interesting words that are synonymous with spirit, including soul. The full list is rather long and tedious, but here are some of my favourites—essence, quintessence, vigour, lustiness, energy, elan, liveliness, vim, verve, pep, drive, go, life, force, vital spark, inner man, pith, power, drive, punch, sparkle, and vivacity.

When we use these words in everyday conversation we do not usually associate them with the idea of spirit. Indeed, anything to do with spirit or spirituality tends to be played down. Think of someone who is spiritual and the chances are that the image of a priest or a monk comes to mind rather than someone with plenty of vim, verve or vivacity.

We tend to experience life through our physical body, our emotions and our intellect rather than with our whole being, our spirit. Somewhere along the line the idea of spirit drifted away from ordinary, everyday life.

It is very easy to over-identify with the different parts of ourselves and lose track of the part of us that is spirit. There is a psychosynthesis exercise that helps you to disentangle yourself from your parts, giving a glimpse at your core, your spirit. The exercise is detailed in the Appendix (page 73), but the central themes to recognise are:

I have a body, but I am not my body

I have emotions, but I am not my emotions.

I have an intellect, but I am not my intellect.

What happens, though, when you have successfully disentangled yourself from your mind, body and emotions? What is left? There *is* something left and that something can be called spirit.

When we think of someone we love (or hate) we do not necessarily think about their face or their clothes or what they say or do, we think about their essence, or spirit.

This essence or life force is particularly obvious in plants and flowers. They are at their most vibrant when they are still growing in the earth and a plant's vitality is visibly lessened the moment it is picked. It is not just the physical process of wilting; somehow its 'get up and go' has got up and gone.

Strangely enough even inanimate objects also have 'spirit'. Some houses have a warm, welcoming feeling to them while others are gloomy and full of foreboding. This goes far deeper than the general state of repair or whether the paintwork happens to be brown or white—there is a definite something, the house spirit, which persuades people to buy homes with peeling, awful wallpaper, dry rot and leaky roofs, while perfectly respectable-looking houses remain on the market for a long, long time.

Anyone who has owned a very special car also knows just how powerfully inanimate objects can show spirit. My first car, a VW 'Beetle', christened Vicky, had such a kind spirit that she soldiered on long after her physical body had reached the stage of no repair.

This idea of both animate and inanimate things having spirit is much more than fancy or fantasy. Kirlian photography shows that all manner of things have distinctive energy fields.

Kirlian photography, sometimes known as electrophotography or high voltage photography, was discovered by the Russians Semyon and Valentine Kirlian in 1939. A high voltage charge is passed across photosensitive paper which shows up an energy field around whatever is being photographed. No light source is used, yet the process shows up a corona, a halo or energy field.

Both inanimate objects, such as coins, pens and scissors, and living things, such as plants and human hands, have a corona surrounding them which can be seen with Kirlian photography. Kirlian photographs show that this corona varies according to the subject's vital force so that a leaf plucked straight from a tree has a large halo that gets smaller and smaller as the leaf dries out and dies. Similarly, the corona surrounding someone's hand varies in size and shape depending on the person's health and vitality.

Enthusiasm for Kirlian photography waxes and wanes while scientists argue about the exact nature of what Kirlian photographs actually reveal. Whatever else is finally proved, the simple fact is that there is more to people and things than meets the naked eye and, as far as people are concerned, we certainly do not end at our skin. One way of experiencing this phenomenon is to try an exercise which is often used in spiritual healing workshops.

It usually helps you to concentrate if you close your eyes during the exercise. Sit in a comfortable chair with your back straight and with both feet flat on the floor. Bring the palms of your hands close together, but without them actually touching. It is a slow, silent, clapping routine. Play with the space between your two hands, keeping them just a few inches apart. Notice how this feels.

Now move your hands as far apart as you can, now bring them closer together and again play with the space between them. Notice the quality of the space between your hands. The quality of the space could be warm, tingly, it could feel like a ball of energy, it might feel slightly dense, you might even feel more aware of the backs of your hands. That feeling, that experience of whatever it is that is between your hands, is different for everybody who tries it.

The exercise is simply one way of experiencing the part of you that is not your mind, body or emotions. This part of you can be called spirit, prana, energy, vital force, even bioplasmic force or electromagnetic field.

I know from personal experience that the quality and quantity of that energy between my hands varies enormously depending on whether I feel healthy or sick, tired or refreshed. But what part does this energy play in the whole healing process—and what exactly is spiritual healing?

Modern 'orthodox' medicine brings in the big battalions to fight disease—it is a bit like calling on your allies in times of war. Spiritual healing does not call in the big guns from outside, but bolsters the body's own healing mechanism from the inside so that the body itself can restore health.

A healthy body fights bacteria, viruses and even cancer. When we cut ourselves, our defence mechanism plugs the gap and then the body's tissue rebuilding forces come into play.

Fighting disease can turn our bodies into a battleground where the body's temperature rises in the heat of the fight. However, sometimes it is such a silent affair that we do not even know that there is a battle going on. Often the only way older people know that they have ever had glandular fever is via blood tests showing that their bodies have produced the antibodies. They must have had glandular fever at some point, but dealt with it so very quietly that they did not even know they had had it!

Whether the defence mechanism does its work by throwing up lots of symptoms or by getting on with it silently, it is still doing its job. But why should different people and different immune systems be exposed to the same threats and yet behave quite differently? Why is it that not everybody exposed to colds, glandular fever, malaria or whatever has the same reactions to them?

Age is certainly one factor. Very young children and babies are likely to get very high temperatures and be very ill for a few days and recover quickly. Elderly people, particularly the very elderly, are more prone to long, protracted illnesses and are more likely to suffer prolonged aches and pains than actual fevers.

Very young children and babies have very strong vital forces, very strong defence mechanisms. Their high energy and fighting spirit makes battles short, sharp and acute. Older people tend to have slower, weaker vital forces that make the whole process much longer, more drawn out and more likely to be chronic.

There is a certain truth behind the phrase 'He's too slow to catch a cold'—people who are very ill, very rarely have colds, since their bodies have not got the strength to throw up the symptoms.

Obviously there are many more factors that can affect a person's vital force; which in turn affects the body's ability to heal itself. Spiritual healing, like acupuncture and homeopathy, is directly concerned with the vital force, it speaks directly to the self-healing process.

It cannot be coincidence that the two illnesses which have

frightened and foxed modern conventional medicine are cancer and AIDS. With both cancer and AIDS the body's defence mechanism has lost its fighting spirit. Modern science knows how the body's defence mechanism works, it even understands how to suppress or stop it with the help of steroids, but mechanical, physical medicine cannot re-start the self-healing process once it has stopped. The motivation behind the body's defence mechanism and all the other physical systems is spirit.

The principle of spirit, vital force or life force, is the stuff on which acupuncture and homeopathy are both based. With these forms of medicine, the main concern is to work directly with the vital force to bring mind, body, emotions and spirit into balance. Spiritual healing works in the same way, it works directly with the vital force. Some people identify it with the flux, the flow of life, others with bioplasmic fields, electromagnetic fields, energy bodies and the like. Spiritual healers recognize the vital force as healing energy; scientists see it as the very stuff that atoms are made of.

Sir Arthur Eddington, one of the fathers of modern physics, once confessed[1] that atomic theory can be summarised as: 'Something unknown is doing we don't know what and it makes as much sense as Lewis Carroll's:

"... The slithy toves
Did gyre and gimble in the wabe; ..." '

This could also have been said about spiritual healing as, no matter how many attempts are made to describe it, it is just as unknown and awe inspiring.

Fortunately we do not have to understand the inner workings of the atom to be able to function in the everyday physical world so, rather than try to grasp these slithy toves more tightly, let us now investigate the nitty gritty of what actually happens when a patient goes for healing.

[1]Sir Arthur Eddington, *The Nature of the Physical World* (J. M. Dent, 1935)

CHAPTER 2
WHAT HAPPENS WHEN YOU ATTEND
A SPIRITUAL HEALING SESSION?

Always expect the unexpected! Healing can happen any time, any place, from anybody, in any way, but just as everybody knows more or less what to expect in a conventional doctor's surgery, so it is useful to have some idea of what is likely to happen when you go to a healer. Before focusing on the healing experience, however, it is important to realize that these can only be rough guidelines.

Just as doctors have their own little quirks and peculiarities, healers too have their idiosyncrasies. It is difficult for an individual's way of practising healing to be either right or wrong. A particular healer's style either suits you or irritates you; it either works or it does not.

Creating the right atmosphere

It is important for the person who is going to receive healing to feel as comfortable and at ease as possible. Obviously we do not all feel at home in the same sorts of places.

Often, there is a beautiful calm and peaceful atmosphere in places where healing takes place regularly. Indeed some people are struck very forcibly by a sense of loving and healing the moment they walk into some healing sanctuaries or centres, but reverend, hushed silences are optional extras and a particular ambiance is no more necessary for spiritual healing to happen than it is vital to find a church before you can pray. Of course the right atmosphere helps, it helps enormously, but what is essential is that *you*, the person coming for healing, should feel at home and comfortable.

In the beginning

If you are wanting to get something off your chest, healers are often very sympathetic and easy to talk to. An initial chat helps healer and patient to get on the same wavelength and feel comfortable in each other's company, but these preliminaries are not necessary and if you would rather just skip over the small talk, say so. Spiritual healing is one therapy where it is generally recognized that the patient really does know best. When it comes to the actual healing treatment, some people feel uncomfortable sitting in silence and welcome healers chatting to them, while other folk prefer the quieter, more reverential approach. Some healers find that the very fact that he or she is talking helps the healing process along, while other healers experience healing energy more profoundly when they are silent.

The most common practice is that you sit on a chair and the healer places his or her hands on your shoulders or head. This initial 'laying on of hands' usually serves several purposes. The healer can by this means relate to you.

At the same time the healer may be in touch with a source of infinite energy or God. For Christian healers this may be the moment for prayer. This is the point when the intention is set, that the healer asks by prayer or plea for healing energy from the most powerful possible source. This is also the moment when the healer 'asks permission' for the healing to take place.

Once this initial contact has been made, healers frequently move their hands down your back, usually down either side of the spine. At this point, people often experience a feeling of opening up to the healing energies.

The healer's hand may then rest for a few moments on particular parts of your body, which may or may not be a place where you are aware of illness.

Variations on a theme

Some healers like to pass their hands over you without touching your body at all. By doing this they are entering the body's energy field and sensing areas that need help.

Once they have established the areas that need healing, they may ask you about it to see if this is, in fact, a trouble spot. Having located the problem, the healer may put his or her hands on the spot or just a little way away from the body for several moments.

What does healing feel like?

Most people experience some sort of sensation during a healing session, but it is not necessary to feel anything for healing to work.

In his book *The Power to Heal* (Aquarian Press, 1983), David Harvey surveyed 151 people on their experience of receiving healing. Only three people in the survey said that they felt absolutely nothing during healing, yet all three of them experienced some improvement in their symptoms! Most people in the survey were aware of some response during the healing session itself and many were aware of more than one sensation. Healing is a potent treatment! Nearly three quarters of those surveyed said that they experienced the sensation of heat or warmth somewhere in their body during their healing sessions. The soothing, relaxing warmth from healing can feel almost like sunbathing. One patient described the heat of the healing experience as 'a current of heat passing right through my body. It flowed strongly right through me and was very relaxing.' Some people find that they feel heat or warmth just where the healer places his or her hands. It is as if the healer's hands are particularly hot and these hot hands can be felt right through a patient's clothes. Sometimes the healer's hands feel 'normal' until they reach the trouble spot and then the patient experiences heat in the area where they are experiencing pain or some other problem.

Relaxation and calmness are also very common experiences during healing. Nearly half the people in the survey said that they felt deeply relaxed, while 41 per cent felt calm.

My own experience of the calming, relaxing effect of healing came as a dramatic contrast after a motorbike accident. I was reeling from the shock, pain and anger of the situation but, when the spiritual healing session started, this was transformed into a wonderful sense of stillness, peace and tranquillity. In fact, I became so relaxed that for a moment during that road-side healing I went into a peaceful sleep. Here are some typical descriptions of other people's experiences of what healing feels like:

'It's like someone doing your hair or your nails, someone massaging you. It's all very nice and relaxing, someone else is doing all the work, someone is making a fuss of you.'

'I go to the healer feeling terrible and come away feeling I'm on Cloud Nine. While I'm being healed I feel relaxed—but really relaxed—nearly unconscious.'

'It felt like letting go of a deep breath, a deep feeling of letting go. It was wonderful to have someone in contact with me, totally supporting and very loving, being there just for you.'

Most patients in David Harvey's survey mentioned that they had more than one sensation or response, the most common being heat, relaxation, calmness, tingling. A few (14 per cent) experienced coldness and 5 per cent felt some discomfort. However, these feelings were fleeting and no one reported lasting ill-effects.

It is well worth saying here that it is not necessary to *feel* anything for healing to work—the feelings come as optional extras. Regardless of whether you feel anything or not, what happens during the healing session can be measured with the help of a 'Mind Mirror'. Although this has a slightly science fiction ring to it, the Mind Mirror is similar to a conventional electro-encephalograph (EEG). Both measure brain wave patterns, but the EEG produces patterns of squiggles on paper while the Mind Mirror produces patterns of flashing lights. Developed by Geoff Blundell and Maxwell Cade, the Mind Mirror consists of a box about the same size as a small portable typewriter and both healer and patient can be wired up to the device. During healing the Mind Mirror shows the alpha, beta, theta and delta brain waves arranging themselves in a symmetrical pattern with both sides of the brain 'balanced'. This is a similar pattern to that which occurs when an experienced meditator meditates. It is what Maxwell Cade called 'The Awakened Mind' state, or fifth state of consciousness. In fact, Maxwell Cade identified eight different states of consciousness—ranging from deep sleep to a state of absolute unity.

What appears to happen during healing is that the patient—and sometimes the healer—starts the session in a 'normal' state of consciousness, when the flashing lights might be random, but this usually settles down for both healer and then the patient when the healing starts.

Cade worked with hundreds of healers and measured the depth of relaxation using the Mind Mirror as well as skin resistance meters. In the book he wrote with Nora Coxhead, *The Awakened Mind* (Element Books 1987), Cade explains that after a successful healing session a patient will be more relaxed yet at the same time more able to respond to emergencies. These physiological changes seem to be the result of the healer inducing in the patient one or both of two responses, namely deep psychotherapeutical relaxation and fifth state consciousness.

Endings

As the session ends, the healer will often place his or her hands on your head or shoulders and will probably say a silent 'goodbye'. Just as at the beginning of the healing session your healer tries to get on the same wavelength as you. This last phase is to reverse this process or tune back into their *own* wavelength.

Some healers will suggest that you become aware of your feet, or even make a brushing down motion towards the ground. This is simply 'grounding the energies'. Just as electrical plugs need 'earthing' to release surplus electricity, so healing energy needs grounding for the same kind of reason. You need not feel concerned if your healer has not overtly appeared to have done anything that seemed like grounding since a healer's fleeting thought might have been sufficient. If you are in any doubt about this and if, perhaps, you feel a little bit disconnected or not quite all there, just think of the earth and your own feet.

People who have never experienced healing before are sometimes embarrassed and worry halfway through the healing about saying thank you and going away. Sometimes patients fret about 'doing the right thing' and wonder what is expected of them. Absolutely nothing is expected of you as the patient—just relax and enjoy it.

Just as there is a time immediately after making love that has a uniquely beautiful calm quality to it, so there is a corresponding time of intense tranquillity after a healing session that can sometimes be felt by the patient. It does not always happen, but you should take advantage of the possibility of it happening.

CHAPTER 3
THE REIKI STORY

When I wrote the first edition of this book I had a Reiki healing from a Canadian called Brian. It cured my toothache, but I dismissed Reiki as just another little known form of spiritual healing. Ten years later, its fame and popularity has spread so widely that I feel that it deserves special mention.

The history of Reiki (pronounced Ray-Key) or the Usui System of Natural Healing has been passed on orally from master to student ever since Reiki was founded by Dr Mikao Usui in the late nineteenth century. Briefly, it's the result of Dr Usui's 7 year search for the key to healing. After an exhaustive study of the scriptures and Buddhist writings, he learned Sanskrit so that he could read the original Buddhist writings where he discovered the formula, symbols and description of how Buddha healed. But knowledge of healing wasn't enough, he wanted the power to heal, so he climbed one of Japan's sacred mountains and meditated for twenty one days.

On the twenty first day, Dr Usui became aware of a beam of light from the heavens that came shooting towards him. Although he was afraid, he did not move, but was struck by the light and knocked over. Then in rapid succession he saw before him like bubbles of light, the symbols that he had discovered in his study, the key to the healing of Buddha and Jesus. The symbols burned themselves into his memory.

When the trance was over, Dr Usui no longer felt exhausted, stiff, or hungry as he had just moments earlier. When he came down from the mountain he stubbed his big toe, but when he held it. the pain left and the bleeding stopped. The first person who he gave healing to had toothache, the second had arthritis—both cured. He decided to heal the sick in a beggar camp, but after seven years he began to see those that he had helped returning to the beggar camp in the same condition that he had originally found them. He asked the people why they had returned to the camp and they answered that they preferred their old way of life. Dr Usui realised that he had healed the physical body of symptoms but had not taught appreciation for life or a new way of living. He left the beggar camp and began to teach others who wished to know more. He taught them how to heal themselves and gave them the Principles of Reiki to help heal their thoughts.

At the end of his life, Dr Usui recognised Chujiro Hayashi, a retired Naval officer, as the Master of Reiki and charged him with keeping the essence of his teachings intact. Japanese-American Mrs. Hawayo Takata became his successor, and she passed her guardianship of the Reiki tradition onto her granddaughter, Phyllis Furumoto.

Dr Usui made a huge commitment when he went on his search for Reiki and a big commitment is still demanded of would-be Reiki healers, which is reflected in the high price of learning Reiki. It costs the equivalent of $150, to learn Reiki 1, $500 for Reiki 2, and $10,000 to become a Master. Dr Usui's first healing was on himself—which is the first stage of Reiki. Although Dr Usui was initiated into the power of Reiki very dramatically, today's Reiki healers don't have to meditate on mountains. Students are initiated by a Master, who passes the energy of the symbols into the student's energy field by using symbolic gestures.

Reiki means Universal Life Force Energy, so it's not surprising that Reiki Healers have very similar ideas about healing to other spiritual healers, the difference is the symbols and structure that Reiki is based on. Reiki Master Beth Holman was an experienced spiritual healer before she was drawn to Reiki. She says: "You use the form that you are taught and then the form teaches you, bringing balance to mind, body and spirit. Its an armchair, something you can sit in and use, it's a focus, a structure based on divine intelligence. The more you use the form, the more power-ful it becomes. It's a life's work, not just a seminar training."

As a patient, receiving Reiki is very similar to receiving any form of spiritual healing—although it is more structured. A Reiki session usually takes an hour—the healer's hands are placed in twelve positions in all, four on the head, four on the front and four on the back and each position is maintained for five minutes.

I had a Reiki session with Beth Holman and found it very relaxing and soothing just to have her hands placed on me and left there for five minutes at a time. At first, nothing much seemed to happen apart from an awareness of energy building up in my chest area, and then a tightness in my lower back when I turned over. Finally I became aware of how very lonely I felt (no partner, parents or children) and I was encouraged to cry. At the end of the session I felt as if I'd had a really good cry, far more relieved and refreshed than the number of tears warranted, and over the following few days I felt increasingly optimistic about my life.

CHAPTER 4
DO YOU HAVE TO BELIEVE THAT IT WILL WORK?

Some people say that faith can move mountains or make miracles happen, so it is tempting to suggest that healing is an act of faith and that you have to believe in it before it can work. Belief, however, is not really necessary. Unhampered by beliefs or doubts, babes and beasts and even barley seeds, enzymes, cut flowers and cells respond beautifully (see also 'Does it actually work?' page 19) but there has never been any suggestion that they 'believe'. However, many people assume that belief is a vital ingredient and because they do not believe in it, they do not try it. The fact that you are reading this page suggests that you have reached the stage of being open to the idea of spiritual healing, even if you may not be willing to try it. That is all that is needed—an openness to the idea—it is the healer who does the believing.

Babies react to the power of the laying on of hands and respond very quickly to a mother's touch. This works in a very straightforward physical way as a sense of physical comfort, tenderness and love is transmitted powerfully by touch. This seems more logical when one realizes how deeply rooted and important the sense of touch is. Touch is the first sense to develop in the womb: embryos react to touch at just six weeks—long before eyes or ears are formed—and, at birth, touch is the first two-way communication the baby has with the outside world, to touch and be touched.

Animals also respond very positively to spiritual healing. Anyone who has owned a dog or a cat knows that feeling of almost unbearable love when a pet is ill and you are stroking it, soothing it, trying to make it feel better.

While babies and animals neither believe nor disbelieve in spiritual healing, thinking adults have usually made up their minds about it, deciding for themselves whether to believe or not. For intelligent, rational adults, however, it is almost impossible to believe blindly in anything. Most people need to experience something before they can believe in it. Not surprising then, that David Harvey found that more than half the people in the survey did not believe in spiritual healing before the treatment. If faith is an essential ingredient in the healing process, then only believers should respond to the treatment. Yet the survey shows that believers and nonbelievers alike experience improvement after being given healing—with only 3 per cent of those surveyed receiving no benefit at all.

Although faith is not a prerequisite for healing to take place, it probably does not do any harm and may, in fact, be quite helpful. Take the case of financial editor Cathy Gunn. It seemed that the more she believed in spiritual healing, the more strongly she experienced it. She explains: 'The first time I was prepared to think it might work, but I was in two minds about it. So when my shoulder improved I was impressed. The second time I twisted a knee skiing and it was getting worse and being a real nuisance. I thought of going to my doctor, but I thought I'd give healing a bash first. After the first experience, I believed more in the whole thing. My knee was greatly improved and after a few days it recovered completely. I was delighted.'

Bearing in mind that it is difficult if not impossible, to have faith in spiritual healing until you have experienced it, is there anything the patient can do that either helps or hinders the healer? Perhaps the most important prerequisite is to have an open mind. The wonderful thing about babies and animals, and even seeds and flowers, is that they are open and unprejudiced, trusting and innocent. It is quite a subtle thing, but I see the whole process as being on a scale of openness. At one end is the person who goes for healing but *really* does not want to be healed and will hide under a metaphorical dustbin hoping that healing does not help. At the other end of the spectrum there are people, babies and animals who are totally open to healing and are simply eager and willing to be well. Just being open and willing actually helps. A healer cannot *force* someone to be well, so it is not much use being persuaded by friends to go to see a healer just to keep someone happy—there is only one good reason for going to see a healer and that is because *you* want to.

Strangely enough some healers can feel when a patient is actively against the idea of healing—one of Lawrence LeShan's students described it as '… feeling as if you are running into a rubber wall.' It is easy to assume that everybody who is ill wants to be well, but my own experience is that illness is not quite like that—it is more like a tug of war, a tug of war where one part of me wants to be healthy, but another part wants to be ill. The technical term for this is secondary gain—but there comes a point when the secondary gain really does not make up for the loss of health and vitality. So when it comes to the crunch, does spiritual healing actually work?

Does it actually work?
Some people proclaim that spiritual healing is the greatest thing that ever came into their lives—despite the complete absence of any sign that it is helping them. Others can witness the most dramatic, miraculous cures, be swamped with proof and statistics and still remain sceptical. The best 'proof' of all, of course, is to experience healing yourself, but this is so subjective that it does not satisfy the logical part of ourselves which demands scientific evidence. My own personal experiences of spiritual healing never cease to amaze me, leaving my common sense and the rational part of my brain in a whirl.

My first contact with healing was being asked to help heal a friend with backache. As I had never been involved in anything like this before I was relieved to discover that there were also several experienced healers present. I felt very hesitant and did not want to do anything wrong. As a result I kept my hands on

19

the floor, palms upwards feeling somehow that at least I could not do any harm because there was a massage table between my hands and my friend! During the healing session I was surprised to feel heat coming through my hands. My friend was better the next day, but what really impressed and amazed me was that he was puzzled about why he should have felt so much heat from the floor!

This demonstrated to me very dramatically that there is more to the warmth generated during a healing session than mere body heat—a wad of scientific evidence could not have made the point more clearly. Yet, even now, seventeen years later, part of me feels that the whole incident was impossible.

Some of the best-known and most interesting research into healing has been pioneered in North America, but a British healer, Gordon Turner, also conducted some fascinating if less publicized experiments into the healing process. He worked with 23 healers between 1958 and 1962 and, amongst other things, found that the life of cut flowers could be extended by a third by spiritual healing and that daily healing could keep a bouquet fresh for a staggering 55 days.

Dr Bernard Grad, an experimental biologist at McGill University, Montreal, did a considerable amount of research with the Hungarian healer, Oskar Estebany in the early 1960s. Dr Grad devised some experiments with the same kind of procedures that he would have applied to testing a new drug. He found that wounds in mice healed faster when they had been treated by Estebany—even when the treatment was through a paper bag placed over the cages.

Dr Grad also experimented with barley seeds, dosed with salt water to impair germination and growth rates. The seeds that had been healed by Estebany grew more prolifically than the untreated barley seeds. Estebany also healed water in sealed containers that was then used to treat barley seeds. Half the seeds were given the treated water, the rest were kept as a control sample. The effect on those watered with the treated *water* was the same as if Estebany had treated the *seeds*. Interestingly, Turner's healers in

Britain had had very similar results with grass seeds a few years earlier. They found that when the seed and potting mixture were treated before planting, the healed seeds popped up ten days before the unhealed control seeds. When only the water was treated, the seeds sprinkled with treated water appeared six days earlier than the untreated seeds.

Seeds seem to be popular subjects for healing research—in the early 1990's healed salt stressed cress seeds showed statistically significant faster rates of recovery and growth than the control seeds. (Scofield A. M., Hodges R. D., "Demonstration of a healing effect in the laboratory using a simple plant model", J Soc. Psychical Res. 1991; 57: 321-43).

Estebany also worked with Franciscan nun and biochemist Dr Sister Justa Smith, chairman of the Natural Sciences Concentration at Rosary College, Buffalo, New York. Dr Smith was particularly interested in the effects of healing on enzymes since enzymes themselves play a central role in the healing process. Working with Estebany, Dr Smith found that healing increased the activity of the enzyme trypsin.

The well-known British healer Matthew Manning has also taken part in many experiments, including work with Dr William Braud at the Mind Science Laboratory in San Antonio. Matthew Manning showed he could kill cancer cells growing in flasks via contact and remote healing.

There has also been some interesting research into healing people. In 1990 a study was done on 46 healthy volunteers who had incisions made on their arms. Each participant was told to go into an empty room and to put their arms through a sleeve fitted to an opening in the wall. Half the participants were given Therapeutic Touch (the form of healing which is now widely used by nurses)—with the healers hands just above the arm, not actually touching it. Both the physician who performed the incisions and the technician who measured the wounds were unaware of the true nature of the study. By day eight, the size of the wounds of the treated group was ten times smaller than for those in the control group. After 16 days the wounds had healed in half the people who had received healing, while none in the control group had healed. ("Wound healing—double blind trial" Wirth D. P., Subtle Energies 1990(1): 1, 1-20).

There's no shortage of research which shows that healing works. Dr Dan Benor has made an exhaustive study of the research available (Benor D. J. "Science Validates Spiritual Healing" soon to be published by Vision Publications, Ph. (800) 332-8112, (248) 948-8112, Fax (248) 948-9534). He says: "There is more research evidence to support the efficacy of healing than there is for all the other complementary therapies combined (with the exception of hypnosis), 56 of the 131 controlled trials demonstrate a positive effect of healing at a significant level. Healing is certainly more than a placebo unless enzymes, yeast, bacteria, plants and mice are subject to suggestion. If healing were a drug, I believe it would be accepted as effective on the basis of this evidence."

But healing isn't a drug, it doesn't work on a pill for every ill basis, it's a general form of therapy and outside the laboratory it tends to have general, unpredictable effects. A GPs surgery in Cullompton, Devon analysed the results of the first 25 people who had visited their resident healer, Gill White. Patients suffered from a wide variety of chronic complaints: back pain, arthritis, depression, stress, headaches, abdominal pains, repetitive stress injury, M.E. and psoriasis. An impressive 96% felt that healing had been a positive, pleasurable and useful experience in some way. One patient felt that healing had altered his whole outlook on life, another had had chronic pains in her arm which went with healing, another noted that his back pain got better (though this wasn't the presenting symptom).

Patients were asked to assess their symptoms before and after healing and to assess any changes they had perceived. Some 72% showed some improvement in symptom scores, while 32% showed substantial improvements. As far as perceived change was concerned 16% felt slightly better, 20% felt much better and 32% felt very much better. All 8 patients with stress, joint pains and abdominal pains reported some improvement. Doctors perception of change largely agreed with their patients perceptions.

Eight out of the 25 patients (36%) either reduced or stopped their medication, saving over £1,000 a year. Even after the healing sessions had finished, patients had to see their doctors less frequently and became "less draining" for the doctors to deal with.

All the patients in the study had chronic, long term problems which conventional medicine had been unable to cure—yet none of these successes count as instant miracle cures. Miracles after all are, by their very nature, rare.

Chapter 5

MIRACLE CURE?

Spiritual healing very, very rarely makes you better instantaneously. Such instances qualify as the 'miracle cures' and these, obviously, are few and far between. Talking to healers, many can cite an isolated miracle cure or two, but most of the work they do simply results in slow and steady progress over a period of time.

Before I became a professional healer, I had an interesting experience of the instantaneous variety. I was working in a newspaper office and a secretary there had cystitis. She asked me if I would heal her. After the healing session the cystitis had left her and she felt fine—so fine, in fact, that she celebrated by going out for a drink, or two, that same night. The cystitis has not come back. I do not know why this happened. Cures do not always happen so quickly.

A surprising number of dramatic cures do, however, follow a certain pattern. The patient often feels very sleepy and, following a good night's rest, feels considerably better.

All manner of diseases and illnesses have been cured with the help of spiritual healing, but just as it often takes time for a disease to develop, so it can take time to heal. With chronic diseases it is no bad idea to follow the homeopaths rule of thumb that it takes a month for every year that you have had the illness. Equally, however it *can* be healed in a flash.

How long will it take before I am healed?

There is no such thing as an average healing, but there should be some litmus test to gauge whether or not you are wasting your time. As you might expect from something that is spiritual, the healing does not necessarily start, end or even touch the physical body.

Spiritual healers, homoeopaths, acupuncturists and other holistic medicine practitioners all have very similar ideas about the process of healing. They all recognize that we all have many facets of our being—including the spiritual, emotional and physical aspects of our nature. They have also noticed the role that the body plays as the first line of defence—and often the last aspect to get better. Healers have discovered through experience that, once the vital force recovers, once the spiritual aspects are 'healthy' once more, everything else starts to fall into place, following a recognizable pattern, what homoeopaths call the 'direction of cure'. The healing generally starts with improvement in the mental and emotional symptoms before there is positive change in the physical symptoms. Sometimes this is a long, drawn out process, sometimes it is very fast; sometimes the physical change happens at the same time and at the same pace as the spiritual changes.

Most healers recognize that a spiritual and emotional change is necessary in a 'true healing'. Reports from patients that they feel more relaxed, are sleeping better, are handling daily life differently or more easily are all 'getting better' signals—signs that the patient is getting better from the inside and this is working its way through to the physical symptoms.

Healers look for such signs as patients having more energy, feeling more creative and feeling happier as signals that they are getting better. Usually, if people feel better mentally and emotionally, the physical problems will soon clear up. Obviously healers also look for improvements in physical symptoms as these are the most clear cut of confirmations that the healing is working.

Sometimes spiritual healing does work most obviously on the physical level. Take the case of Eileen Addley. She had suffered with ulcerative colitis for 12 years and had been under pressure from her doctors to have a colostomy to relieve her diarrhoea. At the time she weighed just seven and a half stone and could not leave her home for more than a few minutes without needing to visit a toilet. She recalls, 'I knew every public convenience in Bromley, it was very embarrassing. 'She continues, 'I'm a Roman Catholic and I prayed all I knew how because I didn't want to have the operation. I saw an advertisement for healing in the local newspaper under 'services' and phoned them up. When I phoned Olive (the healer), she kindly said I could come around straight away. But when I put the phone down I wondered what I'd done. I didn't know what spiritual healing was and I didn't know what was going to happen. It was only later that I realized that all my prayers were answered by the healing that came through Ron and Olive Broadbent, the healers I went to see.'

Eileen's experience during the healing session was unusual—most people feel heat or cold or some form of physical sensation, but Eileen's experience was visual as well as physical. She remembers: 'I saw beautiful colours coming through like a crack in the sky, it was every colour of the rainbow and I felt it penetrating my body and making me well.'

Within a month she felt completely normal. The doctors say that she has had a 'spontaneous' remission, which means that the symptoms have gone away, but they do not know why or when they might come back. This particular remission has lasted eight years. Eileen, who now weighs a healthy nine and a half stone, is convinced that spiritual healing cured her ulcerative colitis. She was so convinced that spiritual healing saved her from a colostomy that she has now trained to be a healer herself.

It is unusual to have a case that is quite this dramatic, where spiritual healing makes an operation unnecessary. It is much more common to see less spectacular results. Spiritual healing is much more likely to effect a gradual improvement over a period of time rather than spectacular, instant miracle cures.

Take the case of 84-year-old Alfred Tuckwell. He has experienced benefits from spiritual healing in most of its guises from fast and dramatic to slow and subtle. One example of Alfred

Tuckwell's slow, but not so subtle, healing was discovered two months ago. After having worn glasses for the past 40 years, he found that he no longer needed them. The optician told him that his eyesight was as good as a young man's. Tuckwell says: 'I feel pretty bucked up by it. It's great, I can see both sides and everywhere. I can drive and have a clear view. 'But Alfred Tuckwell had been receiving spiritual healing for 27 years so it could be argued that it has taken that long for the healing to work! In fact, he says that he has never been too concerned about his eyesight—not having to wear glasses was just an extra blessing. Alfred Tuckwell first went to see a healer because his doctor had diagnosed a hiatus hernia and had booked him in at a hospital for an operation. At the time, Tuckwell was starting a new business and did not want to go in for an operation—he turned to a spiritual healer for help and did not need the operation. He has been going for spiritual healing off and on, ever since. He says: 'It's nothing dramatic, you just feel you are being helped. Little things go wrong, but they clear up again. I feel better in myself now, than I did four years ago. When I was 80 I started to think it can't be much longer till I die, I can't expect much. Now I don't think about death like I did when I was eighty. I don't make long term plans. I don't have to buy things with ten-year guarantees, so it's cheaper. I just take one day at a time.'

One of the subtle ways in which spiritual healing can work is to help patients take a more philosophical view about the disease itself and about life and death. Even if spiritual healing does not cure the disease, it can sometimes stop it from getting worse. An instance of this is the case of consultant anaesthetist Dr Walter Hart who takes a similar 'one day at a time' view of the world to Alfred Tuckwell. But Dr Hart cannot point to spectacular miracles from spiritual healing, and says that he feels that the proof that it works as far as he is concerned is the simple fact that he is still alive.

Dr Hart has been seeing a spiritual healer for the past two years, since he was first diagnosed as having cancer of the prostate. He explains: 'As a doctor myself I know how woefully ignorant the medical profession is of this kind of cancer, there is really very little we can do. Three years is the normal life expectancy after diagnosis.' Although Dr Hart is still not expecting to live any longer as a result of spiritual healing, he is impressed with how it has helped him cope with his illness. Dr Hart explains: 'The spiritual healing seems to have arrested the progress of the cancer. I'm not much worse now than I was two years ago and I would have expected to be worse, much worse.'

For some people, the spiritual healing experience is not a question of diseases disappearing or bones being mended, it comes down to an individual's quality of life. What do I mean by the quality of life? It has to do with *joie de vivre*. It is not necessarily the ability to be totally without pain or discomfort, but it is the ability to enjoy the beauty of a rose, a child's antics or the sight of a perfect sunset.

If you have got cancer, for example, doctors may be pleased when they have removed the growth and given you enough pills and potions to keep it at bay for a while longer, but if you, the patient are left too scared and scarred to dare to live or die, something extra is needed.

At its best, this is where spiritual healing complements the physicians by bringing in the spiritual dimension. Ironically, it is when it comes to dying that the whole question of the quality of life becomes so very important (see Chapter 12).

CHAPTER 6

HOW DO I GO ABOUT CHOOSING A HEALER?

T he logical way of approaching the task is to contact a recognized healing organization (for a list of names and addresses, see page 73) and ask them to recommend a member who lives near you. At the very least this means that you know that the healer is insured and abides by a code of conduct. So far, no healer has been asked to leave a healing organisation due to misconduct—and there has been no professional insurance claims because healing has caused damage. However, there has been one insurance claim when a healer forgot to insert a bolt and the couch collapsed. Healers' excellent track record is reflected in the low level of insurance they have to pay—it cost only £6 a year to be insured as a spiritual healer, plus £20-£30 a year for healer membership of one of the recognised healing organisations.

This is much, much cheaper than the insurance and membership fees that doctors pay because the risks involved in insuring doctors are much greater than for insuring healers. For example, it costs a GP nearly £2,000 a year to be a member of the Medical Defence Union. It would be tempting to assume that healers insurance is so cheap because they are blessed in some special way. This is not so. As healers can only help or hinder with their hands there is little scope to do the kind of damage that would be possible with a surgeon's scalpel or drugs.

But there's more to choosing a healer than knowing that they abide by a code of conduct and are insured. It is important to choose someone you feel comfortable with. The relationship between healer and patient is very special and obviously the more rapport you have with your healer the easier it will be to accept healing from him or her.

Most people experience irrational irritation in the presence of some people and an equally irrational calm and peace in the presence of others. Being a healer does not, unfortunately, make that person any better or worse than he or she might otherwise be—the simple fact that he or she can heal does not make any difference. When a healer is actually healing, something very special happens, but that rarely affects ordinary everyday life. If someone is bad tempered and irritable, becoming a healer is not necessarily going to change that, although most healers experience profound changes in their lives and their attitudes to life as a result of becoming healers.

There is a legend about the wounded healer and this is as true today as it has ever been. The very best healers have suffered in one way or another and, because of that suffering, can empathize and sympathize with their patients and enrich the healing they give. I have not met a healer yet who did not need healing himself.

Healers often find it difficult to strike a balance between caring, nurturing and looking after others and looking after their own needs. Many healers find it easier and are more comfortable giving succour to others than they are looking after themselves and this can cause difficulties for their patients. It matters very much to you, the patient, whether your healer is healthy since it affects the quality of the healing you receive. If your healer needs more healing than you do he will be the one receiving the healing and you will be left without—you might even be the one he or she is taking the energy from. Instead of acting as an energy channel, tired, 'needy' healers can drain patients of energy or become black holes. The best healers look after themselves and will always check which way the energy is moving to make sure all is well. The patient also has a responsibility in all this—if you feel your healer is too tired to heal, say so! The relationship between healer and patient is a very special one and, as such, you are entitled to say what you feel. It is, of course, important that the two of you are on the same or similar wavelength.

There are people who will be drawn to someone they know of or who have a good reputation. There may, for instance, be a wise man or woman in the area who has always helped the sick. Alternatively healthfood shops, natural health centres and parish priests usually know of healers they can recommend.

While there are all sorts of 'Good Food Guides', there is no such thing as a 'Good Healers Guide'—nor is there likely to be one. As I have said before, a healer who can literally work miracles for one person might be on the wrong wavelength for another person.

For one reason or another you might be unable to get to see a healer or get a healer to come to see you. Fortunately, physical contact is not necessary for healing to take place as you can receive absent, or distant, healing.

CHAPTER 7
HOW DO I GET THE MOST OUT OF SPIRITUAL HEALING?

C hoose a healer you feel easy and comfortable with, someone you feel you can trust and let the healer heal you in his or her own way, do not tell them to do it the way a previous healer used to. All healers have their own style, their own approach, which may be different from patient to patient and may vary from one healing session to the next. Remember, too, that good healing is a question of results, not techniques.

Allow yourself to experience the healing and do not talk all the time. It is very difficult indeed to experience anything if you are talking, explaining or dissecting the experience either verbally or mentally. It can be helpful to shut your eyes, and do allow yourself the luxury of doing nothing during the healing session.

Give honest feedback. It is useful for your healer to know what your experience is as he or she can then check this against his or her own intuition. It helps no one if you simply try to please the healer by saying what you think he wants to hear. The most helpful thing you can say is what you are really experiencing.

Ask in advance what the healer charges and what arrangements there are for paying. Many healers simply ask for a donation—but it is a good idea to be clear about how large, or small, a donation or payment is expected before the healing process starts. Either way, remember that the healer's time is valuable—regardless of whether he asks for payment. It is important to arrive on time and to let the healer know if, for some reason, you cannot make your appointment.

Do feel free to ask the healer about his or her qualifications and training or how he or she thinks the healing process works. Remember that the healer will be understanding and sympathetic. If healing is a new experience, or even if you have had healing before and for any reason are feeling nervous or fearful, do mention this to the healer so that he or she can at least have the opportunity to give you some help. Be as honest as you can and let your healer know whatever it is you are feeling. Do let your healer know if something is bothering you or irritating you.

Do not ask for healing from a healer who is already tired and take things gently after your healing session. You will not get the most out of your healing if you dash back to the hurly burly of a stressful job. Be kind to yourself, have a rest and allow the healing process to carry on once the healing session is over.

If you are on any form of medication, keep taking it, even if you feel wonderful after your healing session. If you reach the stage where you really feel well enough to stop your medication, consult your doctor first, to ensure that your drug intake is reduced gradually and safely.

CHAPTER 8
HOW LONG DOES IT TAKE?

The length of time an individual healer will spend with a patient varies enormously and, as we have seen already, the actual healing can happen immediately or it can take years. So much depends on the individual circumstance that it is impossible to make generalizations. With regard to the actual healing session, the length of time it takes can be as little as 15 to 20 minutes or as much as an hour or more.

With chronic complaints, individuals may want to see their healer once a week. In acute situations when the patient is in considerable pain, or in life-threatening situations then obviously the sessions need to be longer and more frequent. In acute situations it is not always possible to prescribe 'one healer every three hours' but it would be helpful, even if relief from pain was only temporary. Ideally, in acute situations healing should happen at least on a daily basis.

Some healers who work with cancer patients like to see their patients once a day for the first week or so. As the patient improves, the healing is reduced to once a week.

Sometimes—and these occasions are the rare, miraculous times—only a single healing session is needed. It is hard to understand how or why these instances happen but a possible explanation of this is that sometimes patients have already healed themselves. The healer Jessica Macbeth feels that when the patient has already done all the hard work or when the circumstances have changed, the patient is so ripe for healing that very little energy is needed to complete the process. As an instance of this, Jessica recalls the case of a woman who had originally come to her for a psychic reading: 'I suggested she might like a healing as well. I'd been shouting at her because she was very deaf and I needed to give my voice a rest. When I finished the healing, I didn't have to shout any more—she could hear! She started to become deaf when her husband was dying and she didn't want to hear what the doctors were saying. Five years later, she wanted to hear her grandchildren, but felt only a miracle could help her.'

CHAPTER 9
HOW MUCH DOES IT COST?

Healers attitudes to charging fees has changed dramatically over the past decade. Nowadays you can expect to pay roughly the same for a healing as you would for any other therapy, although many healers don't charge at all but will welcome a donation if it is offered.

Healers who work on a donation basis literally do it out of the kindness of their hearts. Some healers feel that if ever they did charge, the gift of healing would leave them. Other healers argue that the healing energy does not belong to healers so they cannot ask for payment for something that is not theirs to give. Some healers feel that they will be looked after in more indirect ways than by charging a fee. For the healer Phil Edwardes, this took the unlikely form of a substantial pools win! Many more healers, however, rely on grateful patients giving large enough donations for them to live on.

Healers who do charge argue that as they are professionals then it is reasonable for them to charge for their time. It can be argued that a concert pianist is using the gift he was born with, yet it would be very unlikely for a professional concert pianist to make no charge for playing at concerts. Professional healers, like concert pianists, have had to dedicate themselves to developing their God-given gifts and they therefore feel that people should pay to make use of them. These healers often have other skills too, such as massage or reflexology. Also, as they are 'professionals', they know they are almost certain to produce consistent results. The fees professional healers charge should be enough to provide them with what they need so that they can, in turn, give their patients what they need.

The whole attitude to payment is a sign of increasing professionalism amongst healers. Ten years ago only 10% of healers charged, now it's 45% (based on the database analysis of 4,000 healers on the National Federation of Spiritual Healer's referral system). Fees charged vary from £5 to £30. The highest fee I've come across was £60 a session, but the healer was working at the exclusive Hale Clinic, in London and the fees were comparable to the other therapists that work there.

How much you can expect to pay for a healing session depends not only on who you see—but where you see them. Many professional healers charge a set fee most of the time, but may also work as a volunteer as part of a healing clinic. From a patient's point of view, there is a difference between giving a donation and paying a fee. Giving a donation allows you to express your appreciation of the healing that you've received, and the healers who offer healing by donation do it as a spiritual exercise, they do it because it "feels right", and it *is* tremendously enjoyable to experience the healing energy coming through strongly for someone in need. But that is very different from paying a fee and expecting (and being offered) professional, consistent, care and support. *That* is what you pay for.

CHAPTER 10
WHAT IS ABSENT HEALING?

Healing in general, and absent healing in particular may be explained by Quantum Physics, the exciting world of sub-atomic particles. This is the place where scientific observation meets and agrees with mystical and spiritual experience. In quantum physics nothing is solid because at its most basic level, everything consists of vibrating particles of pure energy, and these particles can affect each other at vast distances.

In absent or distant healing, there is no laying on of hands, no contact with the physical body and the healer works purely with your spiritual self—this is the place where your particles vibrate at the highest possible frequency. If you find the whole idea of absent healing mind-bogging, think of radio or television signals travelling from the transmitter to your home. It is almost as if the healer has his or her own satellite dish, transmitting pictures of health—whether the patient is on the other side of the room or on the other side of the world.

After the initial request for healing, you need not do anything more about it. During one of Maxwell Cade's experiments, the well-known healer Edgar Chase started absent healing at a pre-arranged time. The patient thought he was waiting for the experiment to start but, at the magic moment, his brainwave pattern, as recorded on the Mind Mirror, changed to the fifth state of consciousness, the state that is usually entered during healing.

While it does not seem to be vital for the patient to know when the absent healing is being transmitted, it does not hurt either. Many healers set aside specific times for sending absent healing and their patients 'tune in' to receive the healing. Pioneering research by the healer Gordon Turner suggests that this tuning in amplifies the healing process. He took twelve patients who had not responded to healing. Each patient was given an 'appointment' for linking up with the healer and given a picture of a shepherd tending his flock. The patients were asked to look at this picture and read aloud the first verse of the 23rd Psalm at the appointed time. At this same moment, the healers projected the same picture on a screen, read the same verse from the psalm and then concentrated on a picture of the patient flashed on to the screen and continued the healing link for ten minutes.

The patients had failed to respond to previous attempts at healing, but the results of using this method were dramatic. Only one person still did not receive any benefit at all while eight of the twelve received long-term help from the healing.

Although this research has been used to show the effectiveness of distant healing, it also shows the power of prayer. At least part of the healing must have come from the fact that the patients were asked to read the 23rd Psalm every day.

Prayer is obviously a form of distant healing—and it works even if the praying is one-sided. Dr Daniel J. Benor cites a study of 393 coronary care unit patients at San Francisco General Hospital. Protestant, Catholic and Jewish prayer groups prayed for 192 patients. The prayers were answered and they had fewer complications than the 201 patients who hadn't been prayed for.

Distant healing also works without prayer. Research has shown that mice recover more quickly from an anaesthetic when they are being sent healing from an adjacent room. (Watkins G. K. & Watkins A. M. "Possible PK influence on the resuscitation of anaesthetised mice" J Parapsychology, 1971, 35(4) 257-272). Absent healing also has a measurable effect on blood pressure. In a double blind trial, there was a significant improvement in systolic blood pressure in those who received distant healing. (Miller R. N., "Study of remote mental healing" Med. Hypoth. 1982 8: 481-490).

As the patient, you may experience absent healing in many different ways. You may only be aware that the absent healing has happened because your health has improved. Some people experience feelings of well-being, and a general sense of being loved and looked after. Research by Dr Joyce Goodrich shows that some people are aware of the time absent healing is being sent to them because they receive very similar sensations to when they're receiving hands on healing and report feelings of relaxation, drowsiness, heaviness, decreased, anxiety and peacefulness during distant healing sessions.

What happens during absent healing?

In absent healing, just as in the laying on of hands method of healing, practitioners adopt different approaches, but they do often follow a similar, overall pattern. First there is some sort of attunement. This is so that the healer or healers reach the state of mind that enables healing to happen and usually takes the form of prayer or meditation.

Then the healer will link up in some way with the patient—this can be done by speaking the person's name, imagining the person or concentrating on a bowl full of slips of paper with patients' names on them or a variety of other means. Then, once the link has been made, the spiritual healing 'message' is sent to the patient. This is sometimes done by visualizing the person as vibrant and healthy, 'sending' white or coloured light or by prayer. Some healers like to write down the name of the person seeking healing and leave the piece of paper in the healing sanctuary. The idea behind this is that the healing should continue after the absent healing session is over.

The intention to send healing is a very powerful part of the process. In Anthea Cournay's book *Healing Now* (Dent, 1991) there's a wonderful story about Lawrence LeShan who said: "A man I knew asked me to do distant healing for an extremely painful condition requiring immediate and intensive surgery. I promised to do the healing that night, and the next morning when he awoke a "miraculous cure" had occurred. The medical specialist was astounded... It would have been the case of the century, except for one small detail. In the press of overwork, I had forgotten to do the healing."

Radionics

No description of absent healing would really be complete without mention of radionics. Radionics is a system of absent healing where an instrument concentrates the healer's mind in much the same way as a pendulum concentrates a dowser's mind. The instruments have no direct effect and although more cynical people than I have said that radionics is rubbish, radionics does work.

As a patient, you have to supply a detailed case history, and a hair sample which is used as a witness, to provide the focus of attunement between yourself and the practitioner. The practitioner uses a pendulum to assess the areas of imbalance and what's needed for healing to happen. The form the absent healing takes may be to transmit the energy of homoeopathic remedies, virus antidotes, psychological patterns etc. Radionic practitioners used to use black boxes with dials, which was not plugged into electricity. Nowadays, the instruments are more sophisticated, but they still perform the same function: to act as external focus for the radionic practitioner—they have no independent function, in other words they don't actually do anything to the patient.

Radionics can be used for healing people, animals, plants and soil. Research in agriculture in Pennsylvania showed radionics improved potato yields more effectively than conventional spray treatment. For example, at Camp Potato, Potter County, Pennsylvania in 1950, radionically treated potatoes yielded 244 bushels per acre, compared to 199 bushels per acre for conventional spraying and only 163 bushels per acre for the control, with no treatment. Similar impressive results were found in treating corn.

More recently, a valiant attempt to research the effect of using radionics to treat intestinal parasites in 130 horses floundered on technical grounds. The research had been carried out under the auspices of The Confederation of Healing Organisations and The Royal College of Veterinary Surgeons, and as you can imagine it involved dispatching great quantities of horse manure for analysis. The CHO says that the horses trial wasn't properly vetted before and after radionic treatment, so the results were meaningless.

General Gordon Smith ran the radionics side of the research and says: "The first year's results, when radionics was matched against what owners normally did, were encouraging. But in the second year a particularly harsh worm killer was provided by the veterinary side and this worm killer naturally killed more worms than radionics, which is aimed at creating a balance within the animal. Even so, it was noted that some horses which looked 'wormy' actually appeared to be free of worms, while others looking healthy produced a considerable worm count."

If you would like to find out more about radionics, I would recommend a book called *A Patient's Guide to Instrumented Distant Diagnosis & Healing* by David V. Tansley, Wessex Aquarian Publications (1995).

CHAPTER 11
CAN I HEAL MYSELF?

T he answer is 'Yes'. Most people feel relaxed when they are being healed, so it makes sense that at least part of do-it-yourself healing should be concerned with relaxation.

Everyone has their own favourite style of unwinding, but sometimes, of course, this might not be possible because, say, you have not got enough time or you are simply not well enough to do what you normally do. The following are some relaxation exercises, the first of which is a bit more physically demanding than the rest.

Muscle squeezing

1   Sit in a comfortable but supportive chair or lie on the floor with your head and back straight. It usually helps to keep your eyes closed. Now tense your toes, curling them up as tight as you can, then let go and relax them.

2   Tense the whole of your feet, curling them up as tight as you can, then let go and relax.

3   Tense your calves, tightening them up as much as you can, then let go and relax.

4   Tense your thighs, tightening them up as much as you can and then let go, relax.

5   Tense your bottom as tightly as you can, then let go and relax.

6   Pull your tummy in as tightly as you can, then let go and relax.

7   Hunch your shoulders and pull in your chest as tightly as you can, then relax it.

8   Clench your hands as tightly as you can and then relax them.

9   Tense your arms as tightly as you can and then relax them.

10   Tense the back of your neck as tightly as you can and then relax.

11   Screw up your mouth as tightly as you can and then relax.

12   Screw up your nose as tightly as you can and then relax.

13   Screw up your eyes as tightly as you can and then relax.

14   Lift your eyebrows and wrinkle your forehead as tightly as you can and then relax.

15   Feel your whole face screw up, feel very tense and wrinkled and then let go. Feel smooth and relaxed.

Now mentally assess how your body is feeling: if it is still feeling fairly tense all over, simply repeat the process; if there are just one or two tense spots, just repeat the tensing and relaxing process in the trouble spots until they feel easier.

It is also useful to be able to enter a relaxed state without having to move or make a fuss about it. Like everything else, relaxation takes practice and the more you practise, the easier it becomes. It is perfectly possible to practise relaxation and self-healing while waiting for a bus or in a queue at the supermarket—no one but you need even be aware that you are doing it! Initially, however, it is best to practise the exercises in quiet, private and peaceful surroundings where you know you will not be disturbed.

One fundamental exercise is to imagine each part of your body getting warm and heavy, starting with your toes and ending up with your head. It is important not to leave anything out. Working slowly up your body, feel each part getting warm and heavy and relaxed.

Another good exercise is to focus your attention on your breath. When you breathe out imagine that you are letting go, breathing out any tensions and pressures you might have in your body. One way of doing this is to breathe in 'peace' and breathe out 'not peace'. Literally using the words 'peace' and 'not peace' in your head can have a very calming, soothing and relaxing effect. Becoming aware of your breath and letting go on the out breath is a very useful and commonly used method of relaxation. It is such a quick and easy way to relax, because it is simply exaggerating what we already do naturally.

Earlier in the book we found through Max Cade's discoveries that the brain wave patterns of an *experienced* meditator and a healer look precisely the same, although not everybody who meditates experiences this level of consciousness. Cade calls it the Awakened Mind, the Maharishi calls it Cosmic Consciousness, but whether an individual is in a deep state of meditation or a healer is healing or a patient is receiving healing—all produce the same brain wave patterns.

Putting aside brain wave patterns the actual experiences of receiving healing and meditating are very similar indeed. At a very basic level both meditation and healing are very relaxed states of being and the very act of relaxation is healing. It is as if you are a woolly jumper that has been pulled out of shape by all the stresses and strains of ordinary life. Both meditation and healing feel as if the pulling and straining have stopped and we can feel free to be our natural shape, we can be whole again. Even a temporary feeling of being without stress and strain can be helpful, allowing our self-healing system a breather in which to work. Meditation though can be more than a temporary respite. By experiencing your natural 'shape', who you really are, meditation can give you a personal experience of the spiritual part of your being, the personal inner core of peace, joy and tranquillity. It can lead to a personal feeling of being at one with the universe, a feeling of unconditional love.

One of the claims made for Transcendental Meditation is that it is a technique leading to greater integration of the individual's mental, emotional and creative resources. TM is a method of achieving an altered state of consciousness by the silent repetition of a single word—a mantra. The chanting Buddhists practise a similar discipline by the verbal repetition of a series of words.

One way in which TM and other forms of meditation change brain wave patterns is by bringing both sides of the brain into balance. It has now been widely proved that the two sides of the brain serve different functions. The left side of the brain is good at calculations and logical, intellectual processes. This is the part of the brain that is associated with the 'masculine' qualities of achievement and goal orientation and is usually well-developed in modern western man.

The right side of the brain is associated with pattern recognition, artistic appreciation and intuition. This is the 'feminine' side of the brain, the side that responds to beauty and music, the mystical side of the brain. Both sides of the brain are needed for healing to have an effect. It is a balanced activity. Through meditation you are seeking to achieve a balance in yourself, to arrive at that still centre in your being.

That still centre in your being, not only feels good, but does you good. The effects of TM has been extensively researched in over 500 research and review papers over the past 21 years. One study showed that 2000 meditators over a five year period showed consistently fewer than half the number of doctor visits and days in hospital than controls. The TM group needed 87% fewer hospitalisations for heart disease, 55% fewer tumours, 73% fewer nose, throat and lung problems and 87% fewer disorders of the nervous system. (Orme-Johnson D. W. "Medical care utilization and the Transcendental Meditation programme", Psychosomatic Medicine, 1987, 49: 493-507)

Self-healing for acute pain

How we experience pain depends on many factors such as our general state of health, how we have experienced pain in the past, how well we slept (or did not sleep) and how generally relaxed we feel. Just being relaxed can help with acute pain. But the more pain we are experiencing, the more difficult it is to relax. Thundering headaches and searing toothaches are instances where the pain itself demands so much attention that it is impossible to think of anything else and the very idea of doing any form of relaxation exercise is just unthinkable.

When pain is so bad that it cannot be ignored, pay attention! Literally pay attention to the pain, concentrate on it. Sit quietly with your eyes closed so that all your attention is on the pain. Feel the size, shape, width, colour, frequency, density, jaggedness of the pain—feel every aspect of it, putting your entire awareness into the site of the pain.

Normally, we instinctively run away from pain, it is something we would rather have nothing to do with. The problem is that the more we run away from the pain, the more it tugs us back and shouts for attention. Simply by paying heed to the pain, you have started to relax since there is now slightly less tension since you have stopped trying to run away.

As you become familiar with the size, shape, colour and general dimensions of the pain it might shift and change, but keep tabs on its different stages and keep up with the different shapes and sizes of the pain. At some point in this process, an inner voice might 'say' something or a feeling might come to you or even an image. If it happens, hold on to it as it is your body trying to talk to you! If this does not happen, do not worry as it is not an absolutely vital part of the process. Once you are completely in touch with the size, shape, colour and general dimensions of your pain there is a choice to be made. You can for example, leave it and continue exploring the pain just the way it is. Or you can make it much, much larger—imagine the pain growing so that it covers your entire body, it can get so big that it extends outside your body, as far outside your body as you feel comfortable. The bigger it becomes, the thinner it is spread and the less pain you actually experience. Another option is to imagine the pain getting smaller until it becomes a tiny point. In fact, one ancient way of getting rid of a headache is to put your forefinger in the middle of your forehead and concentrate all your headache into the finger. When all the headache is safely gathered under the finger, slowly remove the finger, taking the headache with it—the further your finger goes away from you, the further away your headache goes. It is a good idea then to simply wash your hands, washing the 'headache' away. The whole process can be repeated if necessary.

Some self-healing exercises

The obvious starting point is to become really relaxed (see page 43) and once you have achieved a state of relaxation there are several self-healing exercises that may be helpful.

My own experience of the first self-healing exercise I am going to tell you about is that it is very close indeed to what it feels like to receive spiritual healing through the laying on of hands. It is a bit like direct dialling, rather than getting a number through the operator.

Before starting this exercise, sit in a comfortable position on an upright chair with both feet on the floor and your back straight. Relax, taking as long as you need to. Imagine a point of light at the base of your spine reaching down through your chair, through the floor, down through the foundations, down through the earth, right to the centre of the earth. Feel yourself anchored to the core of the earth by this beam of light. Now feel a beam of light starting just above your head, feel it going down to the base of your spine, joining the point of light that reaches down to the centre of the earth. Imagine this point of light reaching down from just above your head through the centre of your body. When you can feel this strongly feel the point of light above your head reaching out higher and higher through the roof of the house, through the sky, past the clouds and the stratosphere, right through to the heavens, imagine it reaching out until it reaches the Source, the Source of all that is, all that has been and all that will be (it might be easier to imagine the point of light reaching out to God or to Heaven but it is important that this point of light reaches out to a source of power that has some special meaning for you). When you feel totally connected, feel the love, the warmth, the healing energy pouring through you, healing you.

Another useful self-healing exercise is to imagine yourself under a waterfall where the water itself has healing properties and literally washes away your aches and pains. Another variation is to imagine yourself bathed in different healing colours—blue if you need soothing, red if you want to feel warmer!

Visualization can be a particularly useful form of self-healing after an injury. For example, if you have a broken leg, relax and imagine yourself walking around normally again.

Some people visualize by 'seeing' in their mind's eye, some people do it by smell, some feel, some hear, some people just have a sense of knowing. The people who see the elaborate pictures are lucky because they have got something to hang on to and watch. For people like me and possibly like you, it is not that simple. For some of us, it is a question of trust, we can just 'pretend' that we are imaging, being aware of our other senses as well, especially the feel of our bodies and knowing that something really is happening. It is a question of trusting whatever method of imaging comes naturally to you. I still 'see' very little in the sense of having a screen to look at in my mind's eye, but my sense of what is happening is very vivid indeed, so vivid that I can feel different colours. It is very difficult to describe, but the point is that if you do not 'see' the image do not worry because the healing will be taking place nonetheless.

Finally, try focusing on the picture of the Healing Goddess on the front cover. Breathing slowly and deeply, allow yourself to experience the healing from this image.

After self-healing

During any healing session, whether someone else is healing you or whether you are doing it yourself, you have experienced an out of the ordinary state of consciousness. After healing it is important to change from this altered state of consciousness to an ordinary state of consciousness. One of the simplest ways of doing this is simply to have a good cat-like stretch and/or stamp your feet on the ground and rub your hands together. Any physical movement that makes you aware of your body and the ground will serve this purpose. Washing your hands and having a drink of water also works.

CHAPTER 12
CAN SPIRITUAL HEALING HELP THE DYING?

W e have midwives who help babies with the sometimes painful process of coming into the world, but who do we have to help us make the transition on the way out of it? Spiritual healing can prove so very valuable in such instances.

Michael Bentine, whose two daughters died of cancer, has experienced the benefits: 'I saw my daughters' eyes light up when the healers came to visit them. That was enough for me. I know that both my girls were greatly helped by their healers.'

Although no healer can stop someone from dying, he or she can help make the transition less painful and less frightening, simply by being there. Of course, sometimes miracles do happen and the healing results in the patient living rather than dying.

So called civilized man is not very good at the business of dying. Anyone who saw *Little Big Man* will remember the dignity and grace with which his American Indian stepfather accepted death, saying 'It looks like a good day for dying'. This kind of attitude has been the exception. This said, at the moment we are experiencing a dramatic shift in our thinking and attitudes towards death and dying. Back in Victorian times the whole business of dying demanded pomp and circumstance. Sex was the taboo subject, only whispered about behind closed doors. Some time this century sex became a subject that was talked about openly and death became the new taboo. With the miracles of modern science and modern medicine holding out such promise, it seemed indecent and unlucky to make an issue out of death.

Now all this is changing. Despite the best advances modern medicine can make, civilized society continues to be haunted by death. Of all the modern diseases, AIDS is the most frightening since it is likely to strike at the very people the media seem so besotted with. Turn on television any day of the week and the heroes and heroines are young, attractive and sexually active— the very people who are most at risk. It looks like the pendulum is almost about to swing once again, so that sex will retreat behind closed doors and death will be brought back into the open again. As, so far as we know, AIDS is largely a sexually transmitted disease, it is making people think twice about sex and life—and death and dying.

Priests have traditionally helped us with leaving this world by saying blessings and in their own way so do spiritual healers.

People who have been close to dying but have somehow survived share remarkable stories. They usually say that they look down on their bodies and see the doctors and nurses trying to resuscitate them and that they then go through a tunnel or across a bridge. There is always someone they love there to greet them and to guide them to a clear white light. The white light bathes everything in a wonderful feeling of love and tranquillity. No one who has reached that white light has come back, but those who have been close to death, share this same feeling of 'going home' and a sadness that it is not yet their time to die.

Dr Elizabeth Kubler-Ross who has helped so many people cope with death explains: 'I've had hundreds of cases of people who have had similar out-of-body experiences. They all relate the same sort of thing. They are fully aware of shedding their physical body, like a butterfly coming out of a cocoon. We now have overwhelming evidence that death is a transition into a higher state of consciousness. It's like putting away your winter coat because you don't need it any more.

'Of my patients who have had this experience none is ever again afraid to die. Many of the patients have spoken of the peace they experienced—beautiful, indescribable peace, no pain, no anxiety. They speak of the higher understanding that comes to all at the transition. They tell us that all that matters is how much you have loved, how much you have cared; and if you know these things, as I now know them, then you cannot possibly be afraid of death. '(*Quest: The life of Elizabeth Kubler-Ross* by Derek Gill, Ballantine Books, 1980).

Most people, however, do not share this certainty that their own death is a transition, that it would *ever* be 'a lovely day to die'. Most people need help in coming to terms with their own death and this is where spiritual healers can often be very helpful.

There can be precious few people in the world who can love someone they are close to in a clear, unconditional way so that they can encourage them to let go of life lightly. More often people who are dying are surrounded by people who have vested interests in encouraging them to hang on to life at all costs. Doctors and nurses hate death because this feels like failure. Lovers, partners, parents and children hate death because it steals the person they love. Some spiritual healers can help in these situations because they can love unconditionally, giving guidance, support and help to the person to do what they need to do—regardless of whether the healing, the making whole, means getting well physically or whether it means letting go of life.

Some healers say that dying actually needs energy and that is what spiritual healing provides, the energy to die. The healer Jessica Macbeth believes that the reason why dying takes energy is that it is a transition from one state to another. She makes an analogy with boiling water: it takes energy to convert the water to steam and, similarly, it takes energy to enter the world by being born and it takes energy to leave the world by dying.

It seems to me that spiritual healing is helpful during the dying process because at this point patients are more in touch with the non-physical part of themselves, than they are with their physical body.

Anyone who has visited someone who is dying cannot help but feel that he or she is 'not quite there', that the person comes and goes. It is almost as if a person's spirit is taking practice flights away from a worn out body. Good spiritual healers help patients feel comfortable with this non-physical part of themselves. Healers, though, just like everyone else, can be at different stages of awareness and some are just as worried about dying as most of us and so feel that they have somehow failed if the patient dies. Where doctors have pronounced a patient 'terminally ill', it is particularly important to find a healer who feels comfortable with the dying process.

Spiritual healing is not always involved in helping ill people to die—sometimes it helps the dying to live and that really confuses everybody! Jessica Macbeth is in the unusual position of having helped her own mother to live and to die. She explains: 'My mother was rushed into hospital with acute necrotic pancreatitis, which in lay language means bang, you're dead. Even healthy people usually only survive three or four days. She was in intensive care and I was allowed to see her for five minutes every hour. I had my hand on her arm and could feel floods of energy coming through me. My mother was heavily sedated, but at one point she said, "My God, your hands are on fire." It was the only coherent thing she said for days. On the fifth day they took her out of intensive care.'

In fact, Jessica's mother lived another 18 months and enjoyed all but the last month of her life. She was with her mother when she died and recalls: 'I just sat there and held her hand. Miracles do happen sometimes and it's not up to the healer to decide what's best for the patient, to live or to die.'

CHAPTER 13
ARE WE ALL HEALERS?

We are all healers—anybody and everybody can do it, it is an innate human ability. Healing is an ability that I share with the rest of humankind, but for years I did not want to become a professional healer any more than I wanted to become a professional painter, dancer or singer. I enjoy doing all these things and for years I was happy to give healing to friends and acquaintances for the sheer joy of feeling the healing energy coming through me. But over the past few years my commitment to healing has grown. I can't say I feel driven to do healing, but it is something I want to do more of, I want to develop what healing gifts I've been given to their full potential, so I've become a professional healer.

Having read this book as a patient, you might want to take healing a step further and learn to be a healer yourself. We all have the healing gift, so it is really a question of how much time and energy you want to devote to developing this gift. The way you answer this question will depend on many factors in your life. There are many training courses available for people who want to take healing further and the healing organizations listed on pages 73-76 can point you in the right direction.

I hope that this book will provide you with a starting point, giving you enough information to know what is happening and what to do.

How do you know that someone wants healing?
It is not enough for you to *think* someone needs healing—the

'patient' must be aware of the need as well. As we have discussed earlier, it is important for the patient to *want* to be healed. In fact, some healers will never offer healing, but will wait to be asked. Others will offer healing, but will not force themselves on to the potential patient.

You might think that someone is in need of healing because your hands feel warm or you might feel that someone needs help. However strong your feeling—ask first.

Simple healing tips

Stand straight, with both feet on the ground. Relax, by concentrating on your breathing. When you feel relaxed and centred, put your hands on the patient's shoulders.

This is the point where you say a silent 'hello' to the patient, the point where you normally ask permission to proceed, asking for healing from the highest possible source so that the patient may be healed. This may also be the time when you feel moved to say a short prayer.

Now imagine, as during the self-healing exercise described earlier, a point of light above your head reaching down through your body to the ground, down through to the centre of the earth. Imagine that the point of light above your head meets a similar point of light above your patient's head. Imagine the combined energy reaching up, connecting to the source of unlimited energy, to God or the Source, depending on what you feel happiest with. This is the point of attunement, or at-one-ment.

Feel the healing energy coming down from God or the Source, through the point of light above your head and through your hands to the patient. At this point you are acting as a channel for the energy to flow through you, and it might be quite enough just to stand there and let the energy pour through you. You may feel, however, as if you want to put your hands in a particular place or simply move your hands down the patient's back. Whatever you do, rely on your intuition. You might also want to ask the patient if there is anywhere he would like you to put your hands.

During healing you will be aware of 'something' happening—

even if you are not sure what it is. It might be a slight tingly feeling in your fingertips, your hands might feel warm or you may just feel the 'something' happening—trust that something.

There is often a distinct feeling of 'turning off' once the healing is finished. If your hands tingled or felt warm they return to normal and there is a sense of completion. Now is the time to return your hands to the patient's shoulders and mentally say 'thank you' and 'goodbye'. Also, you might suggest that patients have a stretch or maybe rub their hands and feet to ground themselves, to 'come back' from their altered state of consciousness.

As the healer, it is a good idea to have a similar 'coming back' ritual. I usually find washing my hands in cold water does the trick. It also somehow 'washes away' that deep connection with the patient and I can be 'fresh' for whatever and whoever is next. Running healing energy through your own body has the same effect and does not require plumbing!

CHAPTER 14

AN OVERVIEW OF HEALING PAST AND PRESENT

In the past few years there has been a tremendous upsurge in interest in spiritual healing—both amongst the general public and within the medical profession. But spiritual healing is not just a passing fad—it has a history as old as the human race itself. Many clues to this ancient past still survive today, giving glimpses into the origins of spiritual healing.

Living in Cornwall, these clues are startlingly obvious. Walking around the stone circles, sitting in them at dawn and dusk, 'memories' stir on the edge of your consciousness. At these times it takes the smallest switch to make a direct link between yourself and the Earth. In these places it is hard to imagine that we stop at our skin—the air is alive with energy and the stones vibrate with the life force.

Scientists say that the granite emits radiation and dowsers detect ley lines, or earth energy-lines, meeting in these stone circles. All this suggests that ancient man knew about energy, that these stone circles were used to concentrate energy and that that energy may well have been used to heal.

Civilized Man, left-brained and highbrowed, can literally and physically take off to the Moon and the stars beyond, but it is Tribal Man, the American Indians, Aborigines and people from more 'primitive' cultures, who are more right-brained and low-browed, who literally and physically bring man home to himself. While Civilized Man starts to wake and remember his spiritual roots, Tribal Man has never forgotten them.

It would take a brave anthropologist a great deal of time to unravel all the links between the different tribal people left on the planet, but there are some obvious and interesting similarities that have a direct bearing on spiritual healing.

The witch doctor, medicine man, medicine woman or similar wise person seems to be the essential ingredient linking these ancient cultures. Their roles vary from master of ceremonies to political adviser to father confessor to healer, but the central task is to act as the link between the mortal, physical world and the immortal, spiritual world. In the various cultures, medicine men and women heal the sick by tending the spirit as well as the body, using ceremony and ritual as well as herbs and medicines.

Spiritual healing also has a long tradition amongst 'civilized' man. The caduceus, the staff with two snakes entwined, is the traditional symbol of medicine and it helps us slip from the present, right back to the most ancient times. The snakes are potently linked to healing energy both literally and symbolically. When healing energy rises from the base of the spine it can literally seem like two snakes curling upwards through the body. The Eastern mystics call this Kundalini energy, which twists around the major energy centres, or, chakras.

If we try to understand the symbolism of the caduceus, however, it is hard to grasp. It is the ancient symbol of Hermes, the trickster messenger Mercury, whose wand of office took the form of coupling snakes as he conducted souls to Hell.

The ancient Greeks also believed that the world began when the Great Goddess became a snake so that she could make love with the World-snake Ophion. The Great Goddess laid the world egg, but just like ordinary snakes eggs, it needed the sun to hatch it.

The ancient Greeks celebrated the hatching of the world with their springtime Festival of the Sun and it is interesting that modern man still celebrates springtime with eggs at Easter.

This might all sound as if it is very far removed from spiritual healing, but it is not nearly so far as it seems. According to the Greek legend, the sun god Apollo had a son called Aesculapius, who was the Greek god of medicine (and whose daughter Hygeia was the goddess of health). It is hard to tell whether a man called

Aesculapius actually lived and worked as a healer in ancient Greece in around 1,000 BC or whether he was a mythical character. But man or myth, the story itself is fascinating. Even his birth was miraculous. His father, the sun god Apollo, is supposed to have snatched him from the burning pyre on which his mother's body had just been consumed. He was brought up by the centaur Chiron who taught him hunting and medicine. He was supposed to be so famous as a healer that he was accused of thwarting the order of nature and so Zeus struck him dead with a thunderbolt. Beautiful healing temples were built everywhere in Greece incorporating the serpent and staff emblem of Aesculapius. Sufferers would spend the night in the temple in the hope of being visited by the god in a healing dream.

When Jesus Christ and his healing work became known, it must have seemed very much as if Christ was another Aesculapius who in his turn must have seemed like another Imhotep, the Egyptian god of healing. The similarities are clear, but then so are the differences.

The Jews were used to spiritual healing being practised by Elijah and Elisha, who were particularly well known for being able to bring life to the dead and health to the lepers (1 Kings 17: 17-23, 2 Kings 4: 18-37, 2 Kings 5: 1-14).

For Western culture, Jesus Christ is the most famous healer of all—indeed, some would say, the only healer. In dramatic, miraculous ways he proved time and again that physical disease could be cured by spiritual means. Christ used a great variety of healing techniques, including word of mouth, distant healing and, of course, the laying on of hands.

The apostles also healed and even St Peter's shadow was supposed to have the power to heal. The early Christians believed that healing was part of the Church's work. If a layman was found to have the gift of healing it was considered to be a qualification for ordination.

Hippocrates was perhaps the first 'modern' man of medicine to observe spiritual healing clinically and dispassionately. In the fifth century BC, Hippocrates wrote, 'It is believed by experienced doctors that the heat which oozes out of the hand, on being applied to the sick, is highly salutary... It has often appeared, while I have been soothing my patients, as if there was a singular property in my hands to pull and draw away from the affected parts aches and diverse impurities, by laying my hand upon the place, and by extending my fingers towards it. Thus it is known to some of the learned that health may be implanted in the sick by certain gestures, and by contact, as some diseases may be communicated from one to another.'

It took until the late nineteenth century for modern doctors to really appreciate what Hippocrates had to say about germ theory. So perhaps it is not too surprising that his ideas on the efficacy of the laying on of hands should take until the late twentieth century to be fully appreciated.

The fundamental tendency of healers in virtually every culture has been to place great emphasis on the symbolic importance of the disease itself. The disease, it was thought, was a message from the gods, God or from nature itself, so the patient called on an intermediary to interpret these messages, to reconcile man to the forces that govern him. Since the healer was the intermediary between God and the patient, it seemed entirely appropriate to maintain the idea of the healer priest within the early Christian tradition. But, as the Church became more established, it concentrated more on the spiritual, preaching side of Christ's work and less on healing.

In the thirteenth century, there was a papal decree forbidding priests to practise surgery or dissection of the body and even the study of anatomy was condemned as being sacrilegious. This signalled the start of the division between spiritual healing and physical healing. This man-made separation of body and soul was to last some 700 years. As Dr Ian Pearce complained in his book *The Gate of Healing* (Spearman, Jersey, 1983) 'If only the Church had associated with science, instead of condemning it; if only it had maintained its spiritual temperature instead of dissipating it in theological quarrels, and the pursuit of temporal power; if only it had not fallen into the error of dualism, and sought to separate the body from the soul, things might have been different.' But the Church did not embrace healing, it tried to stamp it out. Healers ran the risk of being accused of witchcraft and it did not seem to matter whether the healers helped or hindered, they could still be tried and punished as witches. Of course there were exceptions, there were some healers who were respected and even admired, such as the famous seventeenth century Englishman Valentine Greatrakes, otherwise known as the Stroker.

Greatrakes specialized in healing tuberculosis of the skin, the hideously disfiguring disease called scrofula. From the time of King Edward the Confessor people believed that the royal touch could cure them—hence the name King's Evil. Charles II touched 92,107 people and so many people wanted the King's touch to cure them that in 1684, many got trampled to death in the rush. The last person to be 'touched' in England was Dr Johnson. In 1712 he was touched by Queen Anne, when he was only two-and-a-half years old.

Royalty, of course, had special privileges and the Stroker was accepted amongst the aristocracy, but the witch-hunts that swept through Europe from the fourteenth to the seventeenth century meant that healing was largely a precarious occupation.

The very word 'witch' strikes deep within our consciousness and so it should. Our modern collective consciousness bears the impressions of years of atrocities involving thousands of witches' who were prosecuted throughout Europe. The viewpoint of the witch-hunters has been handed down to us. As one wrote, '… it were a thousand times better for the land if all Witches, but especially the blessing Witch, might suffer death.' Most witches were poor, illiterate but wise women who helped the sick in small villages, and what tales they could tell were told by word of mouth and not in writing for future scholars to debate.

One is left with a slightly uneasy feeling about witches. Somewhere at the edge of our consciousness is the idea that healing is wrong, that it is somehow associated with witchcraft, and is dangerous, but dangerous in an undefined and murky way. But while the witch-hunts may have left their impressions on our collective consciousness, the dawn of the Age of Reason, heralded by the French Revolution in 1789, left us with more to wonder about. The way we view the world underwent radical shifts: man discovered that the world is round, not flat, that the Earth moves around the Sun, not the other way round. Later on the whole concept of evolution split the world in two: the logical and scientific turned away from the illogical and spiritual.

With rationality in the ascendancy, spiritual healing became even less fashionable. Apart from the wise old healers quietly practising their skill out of the public gaze, spiritual healing kept popping up under different guises, using different names. Enormous efforts were made to make everything logical and scientific. It was very popular to give something a scientific name and so make it scientific! For example, Franz Mesmer (1733-1815) called healing 'animal magnetism' and, in the 1840s, the industrialist who discovered creosote and paraffin, Baron Karl von Reichenbach became fascinated by what he called the Odic Force. In America, Phineas Quimby gave 'magnetic' healing to Mary Baker Eddy, and after his death she founded Christian Science in 1879 to 'reinstate primitive Christianity and its lost element of healing'. The eighteenth-century preacher John Wesley, the founder of Methodism, also believed in spiritual healing, and members of his congregation experienced spontaneous cures while listening to his sermons. Wesley wrote: 'The love of God is the sovereign remedy of all miseries, so in particular it effectively prevents all the bodily disorders the passions introduce, by keeping passions themselves within due bounds. And by the unspeakable joy and perfect calm, serenity and tranquillity it gives the mind, it becomes the most powerful of all the means of health and long life.'

By the end of the nineteenth century, the image of spiritual healing was slightly unstable. It belonged more to the 'spooky' realms of the Spiritualist Church than to the mainstream. Certainly Anglicans and Catholics were more concerned with missionary work abroad than with spiritual healing at home.

Then, right at the beginning of the twentieth century, the first moves were made to heal the split between logic and spirit, revitalizing spiritual healing both inside and outside the Church.

In 1905, three Anglican priests formed The Guild of Health as part of their crusade to reawaken the Church's wider responsibility for health and healing. While the Guild of Health was open to everybody—the Guild of Raphael, formed in 1915, was exclusive to the Anglican church. It aimed at reviving spiritual healing through prayers, laying on of hands and holy unction within the Anglican church.

In 1914 the first attempt at investigating spiritual healing was made. The idea was to decide whether it could be given any kind of official recognition by the medical and church establishments. Given the prevailing climate of opinion, perhaps it was not surprising that spiritual healing was given a firm thumbs down *(Spiritual Healing, Report of a Clerical and Medical Committee of Inquiry into Spiritual, Faith and Mental Healing,* Macmillan, 1914.) In 1953 a commission was set up by the Archbishops of Canterbury and York, composed of 28 people from the Church and the medical profession and it was equally unenthusiastic and dismissive.

Even so, some fertile seeds were sown in the mid '50s. The non-denominational National Federation of Spiritual Healers was founded in 1955 with John Britnell as chairman, Gordon Turner as vice chairman and Harry Edwards as its first president. Gordon Turner, you may remember, was one of the pioneers who tried to put spiritual healing on scientific trial. Harry Edwards, probably more than any other individual, did his best to publicize spiritual healing via his books and public meetings. On separate occasions he filled the Royal Albert Hall and the Royal Festival Hall.

The main impulse, the driving force behind the birth of the NFSH, which is true today, is its tremendous desire to make spiritual healing respectable. The NFSH and, more recently, the Confederation of Healing Organizations have to some extent succeeded in changing public opinion. But the shifts have been so all-embracing that the NFSH cannot take all the credit. The pendulum is swinging. Modern man had moved so far from his spiritual roots and become so blinkered by a mechanistic view of the world, that he discovered how to destroy the very earth itself. Now there is generally a swing back to the more spiritual approach, a view of the world that incorporates both the rational and the irrational, the spiritual and the physical, the logical and the emotional.

To a greater or lesser extent both the Church and orthodox medicine are starting to take an 'if you can't beat 'em, join 'em' attitude to spiritual healing. The Church is rediscovering Christ's healing ministry and even its Establishment is now embracing spiritual healing, not regarding it as the province of fringe practitioners. Now churches up and down the country have their own healing circles. The Churches Council for Health and Healing's president is the Archbishop of Canterbury and the Council embraces most of the major churches in Britain (with the exception of the Pentecostal Churches and the Roman Catholic Church who are observers). The Council's membership includes 38 different healing guilds, fellowships and associations and 15 important medical associations such as the British Medical Association and the Royal College of Physicians.

Within the medical establishment, spiritual healing is one of the few 'alternative' therapies that is recognized by the National Health Service. In hospitals, for example, patients can ask for spiritual healing and healers are welcome to work in the hospital. In the late 1980's, two London teaching hospitals—St Stephen's in Fulham and St Mary's in Paddington started to offer healing to all their AIDS patients. They use a 'task force' of healers who are on 24-hour call. Now 216 hospitals use healing either by directly employing healers or by using volunteers.

The medical profession is certainly warming to the holistic model, which embraces mind, body and spirit, and it is becoming more widely accepted, as witnessed by the formation of the British Holistic Medical Association. But just how enthusiastic—or otherwise—individual doctors feel about spiritual healing varies enormously, being influenced more by personal idiosyncrasies than by common sense or professional training.

A survey of doctors in the Avon area found that nearly a fifth (18 per cent) of them referred patients for healing (Dr Richard Wharton and Dr George Lewith, 'Survey on Complementary Medicine and the General Practitioner', *British Medical Journal* 7 June, 1986.) But even with 18 per cent of doctors referring patients for healing, that still leaves the vast majority undecided. And even the term 'referrals' covers a wide range of attitudes— from the doctor who enthusiastically suggests healing as a useful adjunct to conventional treatment, to the doctor in despair because he does not know what else to suggest as all other options have failed. The 'referral' may simply be 'try it, you've got nothing to lose.'

It has only been in the past twenty years that the General Medical Council has relinquished its iron grip on doctors which prevented them from referring patients to healers or any other non-medically qualified practitioners. Twenty years ago any doctor found disobeying that particular rule could be struck off. Old habits die hard and it is surprising that the Avon survey found quite so many referrals to healers. However, the presence there of the Bristol Cancer Help Centre, which has focused attention on to the holistic approach to healing may have heightened local doctors' awareness about how healing can help people.

In the mid-1980's attitudes to healing started to shift. Doctors surgeries started to display details of how to contact local healers and some individual doctors were so enthusiastic about spiritual healing that they shared their surgeries with healers. Dr Patrick Hickey in Newquay, was one of the pioneers, devoting part of his NHS surgery to healers and other alternative practitioners. Dr Petroni was another pioneer, opening his NHS surgery in St Marylebone Church where patients receive laying on of hands alongside conventional medicine. Doctors started to practise healing themselves. In the Avon survey, 7 per cent of the doctors said that they provided healing themselves, while 40 per cent felt that healing was useful.

In 1981 the new generation of doctors were enthusiastic about alternative medicine with 70-86 per cent of general practitioner trainees wanting to train in at least one alternative medicine technique (*Which?* Consumers Association, 31 August 1981). Today those doctors are GPs and as spiritual healing is such a simple technique to learn, many will have trained as healers.

But perhaps the most exciting development has been in the nursing profession. Nurses don't practise spiritual healing as such, they practise Therapeutic Touch, a system of healing which was first developed by Dolores Krieger in the US. In Britain, thanks to the pioneering work of Jean Sayer-Adams and the Didsbury Trust, therapeutic touch has become so accepted by the nursing profession that they can study TT up to and including degree level.

CHAPTER 15
CURRENT ATTITUDES

Something very curious is happening. Attitudes to healing, as noted in the previous chapter, are changing rapidly and dramatically—so rapidly and dramatically that it is hard to see where these changes are leading. From a clear-cut, well-defined split between the physical and the spiritual, the edges are starting to blur, resulting in startling changes in religious and medical circles. Doctors are rediscovering the spiritual dimension to their work, while the clergy are resurrecting the healing side of their ministry. Dr Craig Brown is the current President of the National Federation of Spiritual Healers, symbolising the extent to which doctors are embracing spiritual healing. Just as symbolically, The Churches Council on Health & Healing is now based at St Luke's Hospital, and their new director is also a doctor, Professor Rachel Rosser.

In 1988, when Denis Duncan was director of the Churches' Council on Health and Healing, he showed a video on the healing ministry to 120 people at the West Berkshire division of the British Medical Association, he said, 'No longer is the church hammering with a feeling of hopelessness on the closed doors of medicine. The doors of medicine are opening, and opening wide.'

As part of a general reawakening to a more spiritual way of life, more and more people are turning to Christianity or other spiritual paths. There has been a general liberalization in the Roman Catholic Church since the 1960s. The most dramatic change was that the latin mass was no longer obligatory and

Roman Catholics worshipped in their own language. Priests were given more freedom to follow their own conscience too. The rules segregating Catholic worship from non-Catholic worship were relaxed so it is no longer necessary, for example, for the bishop to give permission for a Catholic to attended a non-Catholic wedding.

There are plenty of other signs that the Roman Catholic Church is prepared to be more flexible, but it is curiously loathe to make very strong pronouncements on spiritual healing outside the Church. As one priest explains, 'The Church hasn't committed herself. She's there as a witness, she hasn't come out either for or against. She doesn't give her approval, but doesn't condemn it in any sense, otherwise you would discount the miracles at Lourdes and elsewhere.' Unofficially, many Roman Catholics would like to see the Church nurture the healing ministry. Eileen Addley, a Roman Catholic whose ulcerative colitis, you will recall from a previous chapter, was healed by spiritual healing and is now a lay healer herself, sums up the situation as she sees it: 'My Church wouldn't really approve, some of the priests and nuns confidentially approve, but cannot come out publicly and say anything. Roman Catholics believe in healing, but believe only an ordained minister or Our Lady are capable. It makes me sad. I would like nothing better than to work with other Catholics, to give real meaning to religion. Receiving healing makes me appreciate all the teachings of my Church and all the goings on there. Given a sympathetic priest I would love to do healing in a church. Roman Catholics like to come to other Roman Catholics and I think a lot of people would come to me in a church, who wouldn't come to me anywhere else.'

Eileen felt that her prayers were answered by the healing she received. Another woman also felt that spiritual healing answered her prayers. Because of her religion (she is a Hindu) and because of her friends and family, she would rather remain anonymous. She says, 'God is there if you pray. Never mind if you are a Hindu or a Christian, pray to God, God helps you. The first time I came here for healing I felt something had brought me here. When I started having healing I was in a very bad state. Now I feel whole again. I feel people should know that when you come for healing, you get love. I feel spiritual healing is in our religion, it is in one of our books, but it isn't talked about.' She and Eileen each had her own very personal experiences where they each looked directly to God for guidance. Today, attitudes to spiritual healing are being forged in the heat of personal experience and soul-searching. These individual answers are starting to colour the rich variety of opinions within different religions. Within the Churches' Council for Health and Healing, for example, some 23 denominations are represented while the Roman Catholic and Pentecostal Churches are 'actively involved as observers.'

The Roman Catholic Church is in the interesting position of 'observing' the healing that has been happening through Sister Briege McKenna whose book *Miracles Do Happen* has been published in the United States. Sister Briege travels all over the world ministering to prelates, priests and monks, cardinals and national leaders, such as President Jose Sarney of Brazil who appeared on television announcing that a meeting with Sister Briege had changed his life.

Christianity and Christian healing have gone hand in hand from the moment Jesus performed his first miracle, but the relationship between the Church and healing has had its joys and its sorrows ever since. Very early on the disciples complained that someone was healing in Christ's name and casting out devils in His name. The healer was not a disciple or a follower of Christ so the disciples told him to stop. Christ himself was not pleased about this and told the disciples to let him continue healing as, 'Nobody can do these mighty works except he who abides in me.'

Canon Christopher Pilkington, a trustee of the Bristol Cancer Help Centre, comments, 'The word 'Christ' literally means "the anointed one", the one who is blessed with the Spirit of the most High and this would include anyone who heals in the name of that Spirit be they Hindu, Muslim or Jew. 'Christ's twin ministry was to preach the word of God and heal the sick. In the very early days of Christianity anyone who showed the ability to heal was automatically considered to be worthy of ordination. As Christianity spread, the emphasis was put more on the preaching and less on the healing.

Many branches of the Church are in a state of limbo, neither practising healing nor condemning it as there is a wide variety of opinion within the Church on the subject. Healing is viewed by some as an essential part of the work of the Church. Then there is the more extreme view that Christ is the only healer and that we will have to wait for the Second Coming before true healing can take place. Despite this diversity of views there has been a general upsurge in healing circles in churches all over the world and healing has become very much part of the Church. Yet, just how actively the Church pursues the healing ministry depends very much on the individual clergy. When one of our local vicars came to Cornwall, he wanted to start a healing circle, but as a new boy he didn't want to upset his parishioners. Ten years later, there's still no regular healing circle, yet his parishioners come to him for healing (particularly before going into hospital) and he offers healing by laying on of hands and by anointment to those who ask. Three other churches in the area (including the Roman Catholic church) take it in turns to hold a monthly healing service where the priests offer healing by prayer, laying on of hands and anointing with oil to a 100-strong congregation. St James' Church in London's Piccadilly has a thriving healing ministry and offers healing at its Centre for Health and Healing and at the Eucharist service once month where 30-40 people out of a congregation of about 160 will come up for healing.

In the Jewish religion, spiritual healing has also become much more accepted over the past few years. The Jewish Association of Spiritual Healers now has 90 members and there are at least two Jewish healing clinics (one in Stanmore, the other at the West London Synagogue). Rabbi Hugo Gryn gave his blessing for the healing clinic at the West London Synagogue, because he knew from personal experience that spiritual healing worked.

It's individual experiences that count. The only way to experience it is to try it.

APPENDIX

PSYCHOSYNTHESIS EXERCISE

Excerpt from *Psychosynthesis by* Roberto Assagioli, MD (Turnstone Press, 1975):

'I put my body into a comfortable and relaxed position with closed eyes. This done, I affirm: "I have a body but I am not my body. My body may find itself in different conditions of health or sickness; it may be rested or tired, but that has nothing to do with my self, my real "I". My body is my precious instrument of experience and of action in the outer world, but it is only an instrument. I treat it well; I seek to keep it in good health, but it is not myself. I have a body, but I am not my body.

'I have emotions, but I am not my emotions. These emotions are countless, contradictory, changing, and yet I know that I always remain, I, my-self, in times of hope or of despair, in joy or in pain, in a state of irritation or of calm. Since I can observe, understand and judge my emotions, and then increasingly dominate, direct and utilize them, it is evident that they are not myself.

'I have emotions, but I am not my emotions.

'I have desires, but I am not my desires, aroused by drives, physical and emotional, and by other influences. Desires too are changeable and contradictory, with alterations of attraction and repulsion. I have desires but they are not myself.

'I have an intellect, but I am not my intellect. It is more or less developed and active; it is undisciplined but teachable; it is an organ of knowledge in regard to the outer world as well as the inner; but it is not myself. I have an intellect, but **I am not** my intellect.'

At this point in Assagioli's exercise he suggests affirming what is left after disentangling your self from everything else, to reach the centre of pure self consciousness (I prefer to call this 'spirit').

Appendix
USEFUL ADDRESSES

If this book has whetted your appetite and you want to know more about spiritual healing or you would like to receive spiritual healing; there are many people who will be able to help you.

Your local healthfood shop will often have advertisements in its window or the assistant may well be able to point you in the right direction for help close at hand, as might your local natural health centre. Equally, national organizations usually have contact points all over the country and, indeed, all over the world. Here are some useful addresses:

The National Federation of Spiritual Healers
Old Manor Farm Studio
Church Street
Sudbury-on-Thames
Middlesex TW16 6RG
Tel: 0891 616080
(9am to 5pm, Mon-Fri 48p per minute peak rate)
This non-denominational organisation has a nationwide network of healers. It also provides training courses for healers.

College of Healing
Runnings Park
Croft Bank
West Malvern
Worcestershire WR14 4DU
Tel: 01684 566450

The Confederation of Healing Organisations
113 High Street
Berkhamsted
Hertfordshire HP4 2DJ
Tel: 01442 870660
An umbrella organisation for the main healing organisations in the UK.

St James's Church
A Centre for Health and Healing
197 Piccadilly, London W1V 9LS
Tel: 0171-734 4511

The Jewish Association of Spiritual Healers
Mrs Audrey Cain
24 Greenacres, Hendon Lane
Finchley, London N3 3SF
Tel: 0181-349 1544

The Association of Therapeutic
Healers
c/o The Acorn Centre
57a Railway Approach
East Grinstead
West Sussex RH19 lBT
Trained supervision.

Association of Professional Healers
92 Station Road
Bamber Bridge, Preston PR5 6QP
Tel: 01772 316726

British Alliance of Healing
Associations
26 Highfield Avenue
Herne Bay, Kent CT6 6LM
Tel: 01227 373804

The College of Psychic Studies
16 Queensberry Place
London SW7 2EB
Tel: 0171-589 3292

The Fellowship of Erasmus
Moat House
Manyard' s Green, Laxfield
Woodbridge, Suffolk IP 1 8ER
Tel: 0l986 798682

The Greater World Christian
Spiritualist Association
Greater World Spiritual Centre
305 Conway Street
Fitzrovia, London W1P 5HA
Tel: 0171-436 7555

Spiritualist Association of Great
Britain
33 Belgrave Square
London SWlX 8QB
Tel: 0171-235 3351

Sufi Healing Order of Great Britain
91 Ashfield Street
Whitechapel, London E1 2HA
Tel: 0171-377 5873

The White Eagle Lodge
Newlands
Brewells Lane
Rake
Liss, Hampshire GU33 7HY
Tel: 01730 893300

World Federation of Healing
8 Earl Road
Penarth
South Glamorgan CF64 3UN
Tel: 01333 703640

The Radionic Association
Baerlein House
Goose Green
Deddington
Banbury, Oxon OX15 0SZ
Tel: 01869 338852
List of practising members £1
including those who treat animals
and crops/soil.

The Healing Foundation
Rowland Thomas House
Royal Shrewsbury Hospital South
Shrewsbury, Shropshire SY3 8XF
Tel: 01743 242444
Database will refer members of the
public and health care professionals
who are looking for services of a
healer or other complementary
therapy practitioner.

Maitreya School of Healing
33 Shaftesbury Road
London N19 4QW
Tel: 0171-482 3293
Colour healing.

The Radionic & Radiesthesia Trust
Home Farm
Maperton
Wincanton, Somerset BA9 8EH
Tel: 01963 32651

Reiki Association
2 Manor Cottages
Stockley Hill
Peterchurch, Hereford HR2 0SS
Tel: 01981 550829
Reiki Website:
http://www.crl.com/~davidh/reiki/
Association formed in 1991, now
has 900 members.
Recommended reading: "Essential
Reiki a complete guide to an ancient
healing art" by Diane Stein, The
Crossing Press 1996

Order of the Ascending Spirit
53 Morrab Road
Penzance, Cornwall TR18 4EX
Website: http://dharma-haven.org/oas
Non-denominational organisation
offering spiritual healing, coun-
selling and training.

Didsbury Trust
Highland Hall, Renwick
Penrith, Cumbria CA10 lJL
Tel: 01768 898375
For information about Therapeutic
Touch.

INTERNATIONAL ADDRESSES

AFRICA
Southern Africa Federation of
Spiritual Healers
PO Box 2152
Pietermaritzburg
Natal 3200, South Africa
Tel: 0311901434

The Healing Association of South
Africa
Mrs Katherine Lee-Kruger
The Leeward
6 El Corro Centre
130 Weltevreden Road
Northclife Ext 6
Johannesburg, South Africa

AMERICA
Spiritual Healing Common
Boundary Inc
7005 Florida Street
Chevy Chase
MD 20815

Order of the Ascending Spirit
9120 Gramercy Drive #317
San Diego, CA 92123-4010
Tel: 619-560-9228
Website: http://dharma-haven.org/oas
Non-denominational organisation
offering spiritual healing, coun-
selling and training.

AUSTRALIA
National Council of ASHA
Gerry Terati Lyons
PO Box 9187
Alice Springs
NT 0871, Australia
Tel: 08 895 24654

National Federation of Healers Inc
PO Box 112
Oxenford
Queensland 4210, Australia
Tel: 61 821 3922

AUSTRIA
Austria Institute of Life
Mr Bernhard M. Uka
E.V. Department Academy of Life
Horigasse 8/18
Wien A-1090, Austria
Tel: 0043 1 310 49 69

CANADA
National Federation of Spiritual
Healers (Canada) Inc
Mrs Noreen Hodgson
lH64/331 Military Trail
West Hill
Scarborough
Ontario, Canada MlE 4E3
Tel: 416 284 4798

Ontario Healers Network
390 Queens Quay West
Apt 2101
Toronto
Ontario, Canada MSV 3A6
Tel: 416 406 5065

Association of Spiritual Healers of
Alberta
Mr J Thomas
40 Edenwold Green NW
Calgary
Alberta, Canada T3A SB8
Tel: 403 547 1049

ISRAEL
Meditation for Peace and Harmony
Group
Mrs M Charney
17 Kerem Hazitim Street
PO Bx 3380
Savyon 58540, Israel

NEW ZEALAND
New Zealand Federation of Spiritual
Healers Inc
P.O. Box 9502
Newmarket
Auckland, New Zealand

APPENDIX
FURTHER READING

So many books have been written about spiritual healing that it is difficult to pick out just a few for further reading. Here are the ones that I have found most useful.

Lilla Bek and Philippa Pullar, *The Seven Levels of Healing* (Rider, 1986) Contains an interesting history of healing as well as some useful healing exercises. As you might guess from the title, the book also looks at the healing process through the model of seven levels or seven different coloured rays.

Nona Coxhead and C. Maxwell Cade, *The Awakened Mind* (Element Books, 1987) A detailed and sometimes technical account of biofeedback and the development of higher states of awareness.

Dolores Krieger, *Therapeutic Touch Inner Workbook* (Bear & Co., 1996) Dr Krieger, who is a professor of nursing, was the first person to create and successfully teach a course on healing to medical practitioners. It is a practical, step-by-step guide to healing, and is mercifully uncluttered by either medical or spiritual jargon.

Jean Sayre-Adams and Steve Wright (Churchill Livingstone, 1995) *The Theory and Practice of Therapeutic Touch* Essential reading for nurses who want to study and practice Therapeutic Touch.

Lawrence LeShan, *The Medium, the Mystic and The Physicist*

(Penguin, 1995) The chapter on healing is fascinating as LeShan explores healers' perceptions of healing and then goes on to his own experiences and experiments with healing.

Morris Maddocks, *The Christian Healing Ministry* (SPCK, 1995) A very informative and scholarly book on healing and Christianity.

Robert Peel, *Spiritual Healing in a Scientific Age* (Harper & Row, 1987) An interesting exploration of spiritual healing from the Christian Scientist perspective.

Alan Young, *Spiritual Healing* (De Vorss, California, 1982) Apart from being a good general introduction to healing, there are also useful chapters on self-healing and causes of disease and helpful hints on how to heal.

Books come and go—and many of the books which I found so helpful when I was writing the first edition of this book are sadly out of print. However, there's a new crop of books which you may find useful. Most (but not all) of these are part of the recommended reading list from the National Federation of Spiritual Healing.

Jack Angelo, *Your Healing Power* (Piatkus, 1996) This is a step-by step practical course for those who wish to awaken and develop their healing gifts. It can be used as a self healing manual, as a reference book for healers and also as a workshop text.

Nick Bamforth, *Trusting the Healer Within* (Amethyst, 1989) This book contains some very clear descriptions of the chakra system (the energy centres in the body), discussions and guided meditations focusing on healing common problems such as grief and addiction.

Liz Hodgkinson, *Spiritual Healing—Everything you want to know* (Piatkus, 1990) An informative book which describes the many different kinds of healing available and looks at the work of some remarkable healers who practise today. It also tells you what to expect from healing.

Allegra Taylor, *Acquainted with the Night* **(C.W. Daniel, 1995)** A wonderfully readable book which is the result of the author spending a year working in a hospice and training to become part of London Lighthouse, the support network for people with AIDS.

Allegra Taylor, *I Fly Out with Bright Feathers* **(C.W. Daniel, 1995)** Allegra Taylor's world-wide quest to understand how healing works and her own gradual acquisition of healing skills.

Jessica Macbeth, *Moon Over Water* **(Gateway, 1997)** Essential reading for anyone who meditates, or who has thought about meditating. Like having a friend helping you, someone who understands all the joys, problems and difficulties because she has experienced them herself.

Jessica Macbeth, *Sun Over Mountain* **(Gateway, 1997)** A course in guided imagery which includes exercises to help you deepen your understanding of imagery and introduces you to your own, inner healer.

Lawrence LeShan, *Cancer as a Turning Point* **(Gateway, 1996)** This is an inspiring book for people with cancer. It is full of stories of people who have proved LeShan's idea that most people with cancer have an unrealised dream lurking beneath the surface, and that adding the power of this dream to other healing methods may mean the difference between life and death, or between a meanful and an empty death. This new edition also contains a workbook, a series of thoughtful exercises such as writing your own obituary for the life you've had (and the life you could have if you really took control of your life and shape it nearer to your heart's desire).

Stephen Levine, *Healing into Life and Death* **(Gateway, 1995)** This book is richly interwoven with stories of people who have found healing through compassion and acceptance. It also contains some excellent guided meditations.

M'Haletta & Carmella B'han, *Benjaya's Gifts* **(Hazelwood House, 1996)** I've often thought that there are many similarities between birthing and dying and this book confirms all my prejudices. It's a very moving account of Benjay's birth (in a fish tank) and his death (drowned in a river). It was written by his mother and grandmother with accounts from many of the people who were touched by him during his brief life. It's full of love and joy—a sparkling, spiritual book.

INDEX